SUDDEN SEA

SUDDEN SEA

The Great Hurricane of 1938

R. A. SCOTTI

LITTLE, BROWN AND COMPANY

BOSTON   NEW YORK   LONDON

FIRST EDITION

"We Have Seen the Wind," from *Collected Poems 1930–1993* by May Sarton. Copyright © 1993, 1988, 1984, 1980, 1974 by May Sarton. Used by permission of W. W. Norton & Company, Inc.

Library of Congress Cataloging-in-Publication Data

Scotti, R. A.
    Sudden sea : the Great Hurricane of 1938 / R. A. Scotti — 1st ed.
       p. cm.
    Includes index.
       1. Hurricane — Northeastern States — History — 20th century.
    I. Title: Great Hurricane of 1938. II. Title.

QC945.S475 2003
363.34'922 — dc21   2003046093

10 9 8 7 6 5 4 3 2

Q-MART

Book design by Fearn Cutler de Vicq
Printed in the United States of America

Lal,
to your bright eyes

The noontide sun, call'd forth the mutinous winds,
And 'twixt the green sea and the azur'd vault
Set roaring war.

— William Shakespeare, *The Tempest*

CONTENTS

Contents

SUDDEN SEA

Gone with the Wind

July 14, 1938, was a scorcher — 90° in the shade, air like pond scum. At New York's Floyd Bennett Airfield, men in shirtsleeves and loosened ties, jackets slung over their shoulders, fanned themselves with their straw hats. Women pinned up their hair to get it off their necks and shimmied their skirts to stir up a breeze. Anticipation was so keen that in the midst of the Great Depression, thousands had spent precious fuel to drive to Queens. When the sun dipped over Jamaica Bay, they still held their places, pressed against the wire fences along the runway. Maybe there was nothing else to hold on to, no work, no prospects, and nothing better to do that day. Maybe they wanted to say they were part of history. Or maybe they'd given up on their own dream and were grabbing on to the kite tail of somebody else's. New York bookies were giving even odds this one would come true, and even money is better than no chance at all.

At eighteen minutes after seven, a lanky young man shambled onto the runway, stride unhurried, shoulders hunched, eyes on his scuffed shoes, his lucky hat — a battered brown felt fedora — set a little rak-ishly. The way he walked to his plane, he could have been going to the corner for a two-cent newspaper instead of embarking on an aerial argosy to challenge Charles Lindbergh's transatlantic record. From Paris, he planned to keep on flying, around the top of the world, faster than anyone had ever flown. The silver wing of the Lockheed was bur-nished gold in the setting sun. He climbed into the cockpit, slid open the window, and waved, one quick awkward motion.

The big monoplane — sixty-five feet from wingtip to wingtip — lumbered down the runway, its huge aluminum belly filled with 1,500 tons of flammable fuel. Any glitch and it could explode as the Hinden-burg *did the month before in New Jersey. Lifting over Long Island, he turned the plane and followed the Sound. In his breast pocket was a note from his girl, promising an answer when he returned.*

From the pier in Fenwick, an exclusive seaside enclave that curls around Old Saybrook, Connecticut, a slender redhead watched the darkening sky. Over the sound of the sea came a distant purr that deep-ened into a roar. A silver bullet shot out of the west. Katharine Hep-burn began waving both arms over her head. The Lockheed streaked along the Connecticut shore, dipped a wing over the Fenwick pier, then headed out across the Atlantic. She waved until the sky was empty.

Hepburn's affair with the dashing young pilot Howard Hughes was as romantic as a Hollywood movie. Hughes wanted to marry her and he was flying around the world, 14,716 miles over some of the rough-est, most remote terrain, waiting for her answer. Actress and aviator were two of a kind — handsome, high-spirited, and iron-willed. He called her "the most totally magnetic woman in the entire world." She said their affair was "sheer heaven! I was madly in love with him, and he about me."

In the summer of '38, Hughes was the more famous of the two. At thirty-three, he was one of the richest, most glamorous bachelors in America. Hepburn's career was in free-fall. Declared box office poison by the press after seven straight flops, she had bought out her studio contract and moved home to her family's summer retreat on the Connecticut shore.

If Hepburn was daunted, she didn't let on. The movie version of Gone With the Wind *was going into production, and she had set her sights on playing Scarlett O'Hara. The quintessential Connecticut Yankee playing the ultimate Confederate belle might seem incongruous, but Hepburn identified with Scarlett. The Fenwick house was her Tara.*

Hepburn was author Margaret Mitchell's first choice for the role, and director George Cukor was squarely in Kate's corner. But producer David O. Selznick wanted a Scarlett with sex appeal, and he didn't think Hepburn, all angles and arrogance, had any. Frankly, my dear, he would tell her, "I can't see Rhett Butler chasing you for twelve years."

By the time Hepburn received his ultimate rejection, it was the end of September and Fenwick, like Tara, was gone with the wind.

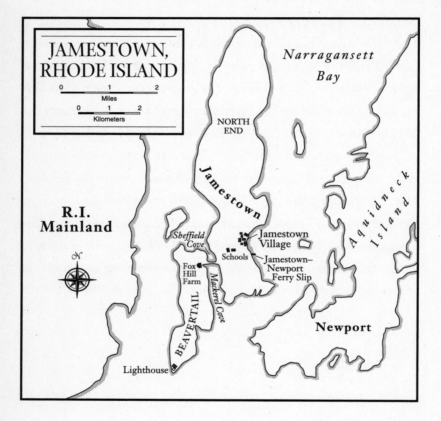

CHAPTER I

A Perfect Day

At the tail end of the bleakest summer in memory, weeks as gray as weathered shingles and drenching downpours, September 21 arrived in southern New England like a gift from the gods. The surf was spectacular, the best of the season — long breakers rolling in, crescendos of sparkling foam, the water temperature surprisingly warm, and no pesky seagulls to swoop off with lunch. Silky cirrus threaded across a pastel sky, and the tang of salt was on the hot air, the air itself motionless, as if time had paused to savor the moment. For vacationers lingering after Labor Day, this was the reprise they had hoped for —a last perfect beach day.

The morning began softly on Narragansett Bay — just the flat, steady slap of the sea against the wooden hulls of the fishing boats easing out of the harbors of Rhode Island at first light. Through a thin morning fog, the sun was a silver-white dollar, promising a bright day. The beam from the Beavertail lighthouse at the southern tip of Jamestown Island guided the boats out. The gooselike honk of the lighthouse horn and the random shout of one fisherman to another carried across the water. Otherwise, the bay was strangely silent. No gulls trailed the wakes, calling to one another and diving for breakfast. There was no birdsong at all.

Carl Chellis, the lightkeeper, was up with the dawn, watching the boats glide out. There were swordfish boats, forty- or fifty-footers with long pulpits and high lookouts so they could sneak up on their catch, and big trawlers, holds packed with ice, crews curled up in the cabins or sprawled on deck sleeping off the night before. Striped bass and blues, the catch of weekend fishermen, were running off Block Island, so plentiful you could almost lean over the side of the boats and scoop them up. But the big trawlers were in the hard, dirty business of commercial fishing. They bottom fished, dragging for halibut, skate, cod, haddock, flounder, the white fish served at the meatless Friday supper tables of Catholic families throughout the Northeast. The old-guard Yankees were becoming a minority in southern New England. Irish, Italian, and Portuguese immigrants were changing the demographics and politics of the larger cities.

Out on the bay, handliners, two guys in a dory working maybe a dozen lines over the side, slapped the wakes of the big fishing boats, and in his lone rowboat, a single fisherman leaned into the oars, pulled back, leaned in, as rhythmic as the tide. Chellis recognized the young Greek — Gianitis, his name was. Nobody knew much about him. He had come to Jamestown in early September, against the summer tide. How he had gotten from Ionia to the shores of a small Yankee island in Narragansett Bay was anybody's guess, but for two weeks he'd been living in a fishing shack a couple of miles north with his wife and two boys. One of those real estate operators who peddle swampland in Florida as beach estates might describe it as a rustic bungalow. Rudimentary, bordering on squalid, would be a truer description. The shack had outdoor plumbing, no heat, and walls like cheesecloth, yet in the Great Depression, four flimsy walls and a leaky roof could be a blessing. The Gianitises mostly kept to themselves, although some mornings Chellis would see the young wife out on the rocks with her sons, a pair of sweet, serious-faced little boys who looked like twins. They were five and six years old, with eyes as black as kalamata olives.

Chellis had two boys of his own. Bill, sixteen, was mellow and even-keeled like his father. In another year he would join the navy and serve for thirty years. Clayton, eleven, was the wild one who would do anything on a dare. He was a seal in the water and a handful anywhere. Then there was seven-year-old Marion, the family sweetheart. Her mother, Ethel, dressed her like a princess and wrapped her blond hair in rags to make banana curls. Everybody said Marion looked like Shirley Temple.

Jamestown is Newport's sister island. The two sit side by side at the entrance to Narragansett Bay, and like many sisters, they share a history and little else. Jamestown is a place to live. Newport, with its fabled estates, is a place to visit. Just nine square miles of rugged beauty, Jamestown is formed by a pair of long ovals — Beavertail to the southwest and a much larger oval to the northeast. A narrow causeway created by a low-lying sandbar links the two. Mackerel Cove, the town beach, is on one side of the causeway; Sheffield Cove, an excellent spot for clamming, is on the other.

Jamestown was founded in 1656 when Benedict Arnold, first governor of Rhode Island and the staunchly upright great-grandfather of the notorious Revolutionary War traitor, led a group of Newport families across the bay. They bought the island from the Narragansett Indians and divided it into twenty-two farms. Arnold chose Fox Hill Farm for himself. It was one of the most beautiful spots on the island, one thousand acres with pastures that slope to the edge of the coves.

Beavertail hadn't changed much since Governor Arnold lived there: open fields as far as the eye can see; sweeping views of the ocean in every direction; and along its rugged banks, glacial outcrops — slate ledges and sea-bleached shelves of rock and shale above the tide line, slimy green slopes below. It is a dangerous spot for swimmers, a paradise for fishermen. The Beavertail light was built at the southern tip in 1753. It is the third-oldest lighthouse in the country.

The village of Jamestown grew up in the larger, northerly section, which looks across the bay passage to Newport. In the Gilded Era, when fortunes were truly fabulous, Newport became the playing field of New York's Four Hundred. They moved from Fifth Avenue to Bellevue Avenue for the season, arriving with steamer trunks and servants by private railcar and yacht. Their favorite sport was one-upmanship, and in the spirit of the game, Vanderbilts and Astors built summer palaces, one more grandiose than the next.

For a brief time, Jamestown basked in the reflected glow. Hotels and guesthouses that could accommodate more than one thousand lined its east harbor, just a short ferry ride from Newport. The poshest spot, the 113-room Thorndike Hotel, boasted hot baths on every floor, electric lights, and a hydraulic lift. Summer rentals on the island soared. Prices ranged from $125 a season for a bungalow to $1,500 for a ten-room house with an ocean view. Some enterprising islanders moved out of their homes to cash in on the summer trade. Such Main Line Philadelphians as Charles and William Wharton, who shunned the gaudy excess of Newport, discovered the harmony of Jamestown and built splendid summer mansions on stony promontories to the north and south of the village.

War and the Depression brought an end to Jamestown's prosperity. By the end of 1938, only two summer hotels remained in service, the Bay View and the Bay Voyage. The others had been abandoned or razed. Still, summers were lively. The island had a casino, movie theater, country club, yacht club, tennis courts, and an eighteen-hole golf course said to rival St. Andrews in Scotland, the Yankee Stadium of golf. At Mackerel Cove there was a handsome bathing pavilion — two stories high and almost three hundred feet long, with one hundred bathhouses downstairs and a ballroom upstairs. Jazz bands played in the gazebo on Shoreby Hill in the long cool evenings. The navy's Atlantic Fleet summered in the bay, and there was the excitement of the America's Cup race.

Accessible only by water, Jamestown became icebound and bleak in winter. Bobsleigh rides, candy pulls, and skating parties kept the youngsters occupied. Occasionally a ship lost her bearings in the fog and wandered into Mackerel Cove, mistaking it for Newport Harbor. The ship would run aground and have to be towed. That was about as eventful as life got in the bare-boned off-season when just eking out a living was a struggle. But this was September, the optimal time of year. The weather was fine, and the islanders were free, flush, and filled with a proprietary feeling as they reclaimed their island, and their children returned to school.

The sun was burning off the morning haze when the Jamestown school bus pulled up at the Beavertail light. Norm Caswell picked up the Chellis kids, then stopped at one of the summer fishing camps clustered along the rocky shore for the Gianitis boys. His final stop on this run would be Fox Hill Farm. There was only one school bus for the island, and Norm made two loops each morning and afternoon, one to Beavertail, the other to the far north end. He dropped off the high school kids in town so they could catch the ferry to Newport, then swung up Narragansett Avenue, the main commercial street, to North Road. Jamestown had two schools there, a block apart — Clarke School, a square, one-story brick middle school, and the Carr School, a shingled elementary school with a pretty bell tower.

Though not one of the original founding families, the Caswells had lived on the island for generations. They were an enterprising lot. Norm's grandfather was the last of the sail-ferry captains, and his uncle Philip was among the first to capitalize on Jamestown's natural charms. In the 1860s Philip Caswell and his brother John, both druggists, moved to Newport, where they met a man named Massey and formed a toiletries company. The firm of Caswell-Massey moved to New York and prospered beyond their wildest dreams. When Philip Caswell returned to Rhode Island, he was a wealthy man. By then, Newport had been transformed from a small port into a grand resort. Looking across the bay to the unspoiled island of his birth, Caswell saw a golden opportunity. He bought 240 acres south of the ferry dock, divided the land into plots, and sold the sites for summer cottages. Another Caswell devised a bus to transport the ferry passengers that swarmed over from Newport.

Norm Caswell kept up the family tradition, after a fashion. When he wasn't driving the school bus or fishing with his brothers, Connie and Earl, Norm ran Caswell Express, a local delivery service, down by the Jamestown-to-Newport ferry slip. Business was solid all summer — best in June and September, when the summer people were shipping their trunks. Norm probably did as much business in those two months as he did in the other ten. Once the summer folk went back to Philadelphia and St. Louis, the wealth on the island dropped like an anchor in the bay. Norm was a good sort, not a man of towering ambition but amiable and reliable. In his mid-forties, a father of three, he was popular with all the children who rode the school bus.

Joseph Matoes Jr. stretched, bending his shoulders back to ease the cramp that was forming, and squinted into the distance, hoping the flash of yellow at the edge of the pasture was just an oriole. It was the tenth day of a new school year, and the boy had been up since first light helping his father with the haying. The yellow flash was growing, rumbling up the road toward the farm. He would have to finish the job after school. Across the fields domes of hay loomed like primitive burial mounds through the breaking mist. Cows grazed in the meadows that rolled to the edge of Mackerel Cove, and low dividing walls no higher than three feet — stone on stone, gathered from the fields and rocky coast and piled one on top of the other — drew a grid across the fields. Joseph started in, not so much reluctant as resigned. It had rained for days, and the pastures were mud baths, pitted with puddles, some as big as ponds. His thigh-high rubber boots were encrusted.

Joseph was tall, a good head taller than anyone else in his class, and handsome, although he didn't realize it. He had black curly hair, soft dark eyes, and wind-dark skin from working outside in every weather. He looked like a teenage Clark Gable, but there was a sadness that seemed a part of him, like salt in sea air. Joseph was too old to be in sixth grade, but he was not much of a student. He didn't have time for schoolwork — or for much of anything else except the farm. So he kept to himself, went to school, and worked on the farm: school, farm, school, farm. His father depended on him. He was the only son in a family of seven. The Matoeses rented the pastures of Fox Hill Farm and the small tenant farmhouse across the road from the gambrel-roofed main house. Joe Sr. and his second wife, Lily, had both been widowed when they met, and their combined families included Joe's three children — Joseph Jr., fourteen; Mary, seventeen; and Theresa, ten — Lily's daughter Dorothy, known as Dotty, also ten; and Joe and Lily's daughter, Eunice, seven.

Joseph's future seemed certain, circumscribed by the shores of the island. When he finished eighth grade, he would work on the farm full-time with his father, and if he married, the reception would be held at the Holy Ghost Hall over on Narragansett Avenue. The social hall was the hub of Portuguese life on the island.

Sometime in the 1880s, Portuguese families had begun settling in New England coastal towns, from New Bedford to New London, forming close, self-contained neighborhoods. Those who came to Jamestown, mainly fishermen, gardeners, and tenant farmers like the Matoeses, were mostly from the Azores. They were drawn by the island's geography, which reminded them of the old country.

Although everyone knew everyone, island life was stratified according to ethnic and religious lines. The Portuguese, almost entirely Roman Catholic, had their own grocery store, Midway Market, owned by Joe Matoes's brother Manny, and socialized together at the Holy Ghost Hall. The Portuguese had a special devotion, and in June they celebrated the Feast of the Holy Ghost with a daylong *festa*. There was food, music, dancing, cotton candy for the kids, and a procession through the town carrying a sterling silver filigreed crown representing the Holy Ghost. The silver crown was the community's prize possession. It was an honor to be chosen to keep the crown through the year.

Except for the Portuguese, most of Jamestown's year-round residents were WASPs, many descended from the founding families. They were land-rich and cash-poor, and like Norm Caswell, they got through the off-season on the money they made from the summer trade. As one of them put it, "We were awful glad to see the summer folk come in June, and we were awful glad to see them go in September." Like most coastal towns of southern New England during the tough Depression era, Jamestown had three groups: the haves, who were the summer people; the have-nots, the year-round people; and the dirt-poor.

The school bus pulled up beside the Matoes house at Fox Hill Farm and the three girls trooped out. Waving to Norm, Joseph crossed the road and went into the barn to take off his boots. He could hear his stepmother yelling at him to hurry up; he was making his sisters late for school.

Lily Matoes was always yelling at her stepchildren. Her features were as sharp as her voice, and her hair was witch-black. Joseph and his sisters Mary and Theresa took care of one another and kept out of their stepmother's way as much as they could. It was hardest for Mary, seventeen and home all day working in the house. Mary had been a straight-A student, at the top of her class in grammar school, but Lily didn't believe a girl needed more schooling. She wouldn't allow Mary to go on to high school and couldn't see any reason to waste good money on a graduation dress. Mary's aunts had intervened, and she graduated in a white dress worn the year before by a cousin. It was a bittersweet day.

Mary remembered their mother clearly. Joseph was only five when she died. In his imagination, Rose was as beautiful as her name. He liked to picture her at the back door, calling him in for supper, her voice as light as a summer breeze, or leaning over his bed to kiss him good night, her hand on his forehead, pushing his hair back. All he had were fragments — a touch, a look, an endearment. They could have been dreams as easily as true memories. Although her absence was a permanent part of each day, he was never sure whether he was remembering his mother or the stories Mary told him.

Joseph stopped at the pump to wash his hands and throw some water on his face, then climbed on the bus, tired before the school day had begun. His sisters were sitting together. Theresa was the prettiest girl in the sixth grade — everyone said she looked like Rose — and Dotty was as bright as the morning in a new red skirt and white blouse. Eunice, still the baby at seven, was sitting with Marion Chellis. They looked like Rose Red and Snow White. The two little Greek boys, Constantine and John Gianitis, sat together in the front seat, silent and solemn-faced. They knew only a few words of English. Clayton Chellis was sprawled across the backseat with his brother, Bill. Clayton, Joseph, Theresa, and Dorothy were all in the sixth grade. Clayton was the ringleader of the boys, a hellion and utterly fearless, not a nerve in his body.

Norm Caswell pulled a U-turn. The sweet smell of the newly cut hay trailed the school bus as it rolled back down the farm road, and mixed with the sea smells rising from Mackerel Cove. As the bus turned from Fox Hill Farm onto the causeway that links the two parts of the island, long swells were forming far out in Narragansett Bay and bright sunshine shimmered off the roof of the beach pavilion. School should be forbidden on such a perfect day.

———

At the western point of Rhode Island, along Napatree, a pair of sandpipers raced the tide, darting after the ebbing water, skittering in and out so fast their black stick legs blurred like lines of ink, so light their feet left only scratch marks on the sand. The westernmost spit of land in Rhode Island, Napatree is a scythe of barrier beach that juts from the tony resort of Watch Hill, its face to the open Atlantic, its back to Little Narragansett Bay. At the eastern end a breakwater protects the yacht club and beach club, and in the distance the Watch Hill estates rise like summer castles. In 1938 a rocky beach and abandoned fort guarded the far point, and curving west from the fort stretched another mile or so of open beach that residents called the sand spit.

Lillian Tetlow and Jack Kinney trailed the pipers, walking hand in hand at the edge of the surf. Lillian was seventeen, small-boned and delicate. She had been born in England and retained the suggestion of an accent, although her family had emigrated when she was a child. Jack was twenty-three, a shade under six feet, with good shoulders and a smile that said she was the only girl in the world for him.

Lillian had never been to Napatree before, and she turned back to admire the row of summer houses that lined the beach, thirty-nine strong, as gracious if not quite as splendid as their Watch Hill neighbors. They were two and three stories of weathered shingles, their broad front porches a few strides from the Atlantic. Cement walls, three, maybe four feet high, protected them from the sea's darker moods. On the bay side across the single narrow blacktop called Fort Road, a private dock extended behind almost every house. The younger children practiced swimming by paddling from one dock to the next.

Lillian and Jack strolled toward the western point. Beyond, where the beach crested, dune grass swayed in the freshening breeze. The sun was high, and at the horizon, slivers of light reached down, touching the single sail that sat off the point and the buoy that marked the bay entrance. They passed a couple of clammers on their way out, brothers-in-law from Pawcatuck, their big buckets almost full of quahogs and littlenecks. Otherwise, they had the beach to themselves. The sea was running high. Long rollers formed far out and swept in, crashing onto the beach. Lillian and Jack darted in and out of the breakers like the birds, splashing water at each other and shrieking when a shower of spray caught them, young lovers on a sandy beach, whiling away a perfect September day.

Napatree felt like a private place they had wandered into. It was exclusively a summer colony, and half the houses were shuttered for the season. The rest would be closing in the next week or so. By October, an off-season melancholy would settle over the place. This morning, though, the water was warm, the combers long and smooth. Clothes snapped on a line behind one house. A solitary beach umbrella stuck up from the sand in front of another. A pair of small boats scooted down the bay. The shouts of the boys in the second boat carried on the wind.

Geoffrey Moore Jr. flew along Little Narragansett Bay, whooping and laughing, oars high in the air. Except for an occasional thump, the rowboat skimmed the surface, barely touching the water. A sailboat zipped along just ahead, pushed by a quickening southeast wind. He leaned out of the rowboat, brandishing an oar, and tried to snag it. The sailboat — which belonged to his sister Anne — had broken loose from its mooring behind the house. Geoffrey saw it go. He had been talking to Andy Pupillo, a Westerly boy who worked for the Moores, and the two raced down to the dock, jumped in the rowboat, and gave chase.

Geoffrey's hair, tousled and sun-streaked, snapped in his eyes. He pushed it back and made another stab at the sailboat. The wind was carrying them so fast he didn't have to row, but the sailboat, usually cumbersome and slow, was empty and moving faster, just out of reach. Andy hollered that Geoffrey would capsize them if he wasn't careful. The boy laughed and lunged again. He was thirteen years old, small for his age but fast and agile, and in that place on that day, he seemed the quintessential golden boy — blue eyes, face lightly freckled, smooth bare chest tanned a deep brown, a strong swimmer and skilled sailor as easy on the water as he was on land, a natural athlete, eldest child and only son.

On that Wednesday his future seemed certain. He would return to the Canterbury School in New Milford, Connecticut, at the end of the week to start the second form. A half-packed steamer trunk sat in the corner of his room at Napatree, filled with the requirements of prep school: one dozen white button-down oxford-cloth shirts, one navy blazer, three pairs of dark flannel trousers, six neckties, etc. From prep school, he would go on to college, then join the family business like his father, his uncles, and his grandfather. George C. Moore Co., manufacturer of elastic webbing for everything from ladies' underwear to golf balls and gas masks, was located in Westerly, Rhode Island.

Just six miles apart geographically, Westerly and Napatree–Watch Hill were poles apart in every other way. Named because of its location at the state's western border, Westerly is a small city with a romantic history and a couple of natural assets.

The town's first settlers — John Babcock and Mary Lawton, his boss's daughter — are Westerly's own Romeo and Juliet. Forbidden to marry by Mary's father, the young lovers eloped from Newport and made the risky ocean sail around Narragansett in an open boat. They arrived on the east bank of the Pawcatuck River in 1643. Their son James was the first white baby born in Westerly, and more than four hundred years later, it is still Babcock country. Westerly has the Babcock House, Babcock School, Babcock Cemetery, and the ballad of John and Mary's romantic flight, attributed to the most famous of all poets after Shakespeare — Anonymous:

> *The bark rode on the ocean lone*
> *And precious was the freight,*
> *Two loving souls transfused in one*
> *With bounding hope elate.*

Two hundred years have sped apace
And wrought in man's behoof;
And thousands now their lineage trace
To John and Mary's roofe.

The first of Westerly's natural assets is bluish granite, considered by many to have the finest texture in the world. In the nineteenth century when the Smith Granite Company, Westerly's first and largest quarry, was buzzing, skilled stonecutters from northern Italy were imported to carve Civil War monuments and gravestones. Eighty percent of the memorials for both Yankee and Confederate soldiers are built of Westerly blue granite, and the masons who carved them established the roots of an Italian community that remains strong to this day. Westerly's other natural asset is the Pawcatuck River, which allowed mills to flourish.

George C. Moore, Geoffrey's grandfather, arrived in town at the start of the century. He was an Englishman who had deserted his horse artillery regiment and fled to America. Oversize in all things except height, Moore was a man of quick wits (he filed almost as many patents as Thomas Edison) and quick fists. Being packed into steerage with hundreds of other fugitives and optimists did nothing to curb his temper, and before he reached the end of the gangplank, he was brawling with a fellow passenger twice his size. An English gentleman, embarking from a first-class cabin, witnessed the fisticuffs and hired Moore as a bodyguard. The two toured the Wild West together.

When he came back East, Moore worked in various New England towns as a weaver, finally settling in Westerly about 1912. He was in his early thirties by then, a widower with five children and enough capital saved up to invest in a small mill. He also invested in a horse and buggy and set about to win the affections of Elizabeth Fahey, an Irish bricklayer's daughter. Elizabeth was just as feisty as George and several inches taller. To offset her natural advantage, Moore wore high-heeled shoes. In their later years, after her husband had made a fortune, Elizabeth liked to keep him in check by saying that she married him because he was the only young man with his own buggy, and since her other serious suitor was a man with one leg, George seemed a catch by comparison.

Elizabeth and George had four sons: Thomas, Harold, Geoffrey, and Cyril. Their father put them to work in the mill as soon as they were big enough to operate the equipment. Elastic webbing was in demand as a substitute for whalebones in ladies' corsets, and George C. Moore Co. prospered. The First World War brought a further business boom, because the same elastic webbing that gave a woman an hourglass figure made gas masks a snug fit. By 1938, the Moores were the wealthiest family in Westerly. They lived in splendor in Elmore, a mansion built by Stanford White on a private street named Moore Lane. Two of George's sons, Jeff and Cy, built summer homes on nearby Napatree.

A summer idyll on the very edge of the ocean, Napatree was "sunshine, surf, and salt air blown over a thousand miles of open sea." Those who lived there called it heaven on earth. They came back summer after summer, the well-to-do with live-in help, and their children grew up, married, and returned with their children. They surf-cast for flatfish from the rocks at the point, raced one another in their sailboats on Little Narragansett Bay, and occasionally lamented the fact that in all the years they'd been coming to Napatree, they'd never weathered a real lollapalooza of a storm.

Hurricane was a foreign word in New England. People didn't know how to pronounce it. They didn't know what it meant, and whatever it meant, they were sure it couldn't happen to them, until September 21, 1938. On that last perfect beach day, a maverick storm sprinted a mile a minute up the Atlantic seaboard. Like a giant Cyclops, the storm had a single, intense, sky blue eye, and it was fixed on New England.

An extreme hurricane is both the most spectacular show on earth and the deadliest. By comparison, the atom bomb is a firecracker on the Fourth of July. Scientists estimate its force variously as the equivalent of an H-bomb going off every sixty seconds or three ten-megaton bombs exploding every hour. The Great Hurricane of 1938 was just such an extreme storm. According to the National Oceanic and Atmospheric Administration, it was one of the ten "storms of the century" and the most violent and destructive natural disaster in New England history.

Most hurricanes attack with three weapons: swirling winds so strong that chickens are plucked clean of their feathers, rain so heavy that it turns tributaries into rampaging Mississippis, and waves so high that at first glance they may look like a fogbank rolling in. The Great Hurricane of 1938 had a fourth weapon: surprise.

On that capricious Wednesday at the ragtag end of summer, a strange yellow light came off the ocean and an eerie siren filled the air like a wordless chantey. In the next instant, serene bays became swirling cauldrons, and everything moored and unmoored was picked up and whipped in — fishing tackle, teapots, corsets, porch gliders, picnic baskets, bathing caps, clamming rakes, washboards, front doors, barn doors, car doors, sand pails and shovels, sandpipers, sea horses, girls in summer dresses, men in flannel trousers, lovers on an empty beach, children in their innocence. Joseph Matoes and his three sisters on the Jamestown school bus, Geoffrey Moore and his three sisters in their Napatree beach house were scooped up and tossed into the maelstrom.

Although the sea had been running high and small-craft warnings were in effect, as late as midafternoon there would be no alert that a killer storm was prowling the coast. Rampaging through seven states in seven hours, it would rip up the famous boardwalk in Atlantic City, flood the Connecticut River Valley, and turn downtown Providence into a seventeen-foot lake.

At two o'clock the swath of coastline from Cape May to Maine was one of the wealthiest and most populous in the world. By evening, it would be desolate. The Great Hurricane of 1938 was more than a storm. It was the end of a world.

CHAPTER 2

The Way It Was

William Stoughton, a judge at the Salem witch trials, once pronounced, "The Lord's promise and expectation of great things have singled out New Englanders." In 1938, even with the Depression dragging the region down like an undertow, few dyed-in-the-wool Yankees would have disputed the sentiment. Back then, New England was as much a cultural region as a geographic one. Independence and integrity were prized virtues, with modesty a close third. New Englanders rarely tooted their own horn. They felt no need to, because, to them, everyone else in the country was an upstart. They were confident in their superiority, certain that they had the highest principles, the richest culture, and the finest schools.

In New England, where both coast and character were rock-ribbed, history was alive and fiercely guarded. New England was the cradle of liberty, birthplace of the Puritan work ethic, home of the Republican cloth coat, and source of the original lobster salad roll (in a toasted hot-dog bun with no celery and just enough mayonnaise). Unlike the prairie states that seem to go on and on, or the big skies of the West, the region is physically compact. This gave it cohesion, or the illusion of cohesion. In the thirties, the farmer-poet Robert Frost, a Californian by birth, was making a literary business out of personifying the authentic Yankee. The reality was somewhat different from the poetry. The stereotypical New Englander, a person of few words and fewer emotions, was only one side of the regional character. New England had produced rabble-rousing Sam Adams, who goaded the somewhat complacent colonies into rebellion, as well as the Puritan fire-and-brimstone preachers Increase and Cotton Mather. The March sisters and Ethan Frome were fashioned from the same soil. The Yankee peddler, a master hoodwinker, and the upright Yank, straight-spoken and unflinching, were both homegrown. New England was gritty factory towns as well as manicured village commons, the "dark satanic mills" of William Blake as well as the *Saturday Evening Post* covers of Norman Rockwell, the pure lines of white clapboard churches set against maples and oaks in brilliant foliage.

The industrialization of the Northeast dated from 1793, when Samuel Slater opened the first successful cotton-spinning mill in Pawtucket, Rhode Island. Manufacturing soon joined fishing and shipbuilding as the area's leading industries. By the 1930s, just about every American was dressed in cotton woven in New England towns and stepped out in shoes manufactured there. Most of the workers who labored in the textile and leather factories were immigrants straight off the boat.

Although such affluent enclaves as Napatree and Watch Hill went on much as they always had, by 1938 New England's mills and quarries were staggering.

For the haves, the thirties were a time of afternoon tea dances, waiters in swallowtail coats, and gleaming soda fountains with mirrored walls and marble counters. For the have-nots, there were poor farms, orphan asylums, and unthinking prejudice. Blacks were called "inkspots," and the upper balcony of movie theaters was referred to as "nigger heaven." Telephones were mostly party lines, and although TWA's *Sky Chief* was offering the first cross-continental flight from Los Angeles to New York, most people still thought flying was for the birds. If their destination was Europe, they traveled by transatlantic steamer, and it could take better than a week to make the crossing. There were almost no televisions then.

Newsboys hawked papers, shouting the day's headlines from street corners. A paper cost two cents, and most cities of any size had two. New York City had more than half a dozen papers. There were no freeways, either, no frozen or fast foods, and no supermarkets. Butchers in straw boaters and bloody aprons, sawdust on their meat market floors, cut up sides of beef while the customer waited. Ballpoint pens, nylon stockings, and the forty-hour week were just coming in. Night ball games were a novelty, and air-conditioning a rarity. In New England striped awnings kept out the summer heat and storm windows kept out the winter cold.

Banks were vaulting stone edifices, hushed sanctuaries for savings scrimped from a twenty-five-cents-an-hour minimum wage, if you were fortunate enough to be earning a paycheck. One in four workers was unemployed. But if you happened to have a quarter, you could buy four pounds of mackerel. For another nickel, you could pick up two packs of Lucky Strikes. In those days, lighting a woman's cigarette was tantamount to an act of seduction. If she inhaled, you could book a room with a private bath and radio at the Hotel Taft in New York City for $2.50, or cruise the Caribbean for $10 a day.

If you were one of the millions looking for work, you might ride the rails south. It could take a week to reach the Keys from

New York. If, on the other hand, you were one of the lucky few who managed to keep your shirt through the crash, you wouldn't make the trip to Florida until January or February, when winter settled into the Northeast, and then you'd have a couple of comfortable options.

If you had a sturdy car, a Lincoln, say, or a Pierce-Arrow, you might drive yourself, flying down the two-lane blacktop roads, pushing forty-five miles an hour with the accelerator to the floor, and stopping overnight every three hundred miles or so — Westerly to New York; New York to Richmond; Richmond to Pinehurst, North Carolina; Pinehurst to Sea Island, or maybe St. Augustine. Then on to Palm Beach or St. Petersburg. Getting there was half the adventure.

Another option was to put the Lincoln on a flatbed railcar and book a drawing room on the *Southern Flyer*. If you were headed to Florida for the season, you would probably stay at the palatial new Breakers Hotel in Palm Beach or the Vinoy Park in St. Petersburg. Days filled with sun, golf, and tennis would meld into gossamer nights. Everyone dressed for dinner — the gentlemen in tuxedos, the ladies in evening gowns — and after dinner there might be a rubber of bridge, an excursion to the dog races, or dancing in the moonlight to the mellow music of Meyer Davis and His Society Orchestra. The other drawing card was spring training. The Yankees trained in St. Pete's, and you could stroll over to the sandlot any afternoon, push open the gate, and take a seat in the bleachers. No ticket needed and admission was free. You might catch Lou Gehrig coming to the plate. 'Thirty-eight would be his last full season, and there was a kid in center field named DiMaggio who was really something.

The Boston Braves were over in Sanford. The central Florida town was so sleepy, it only woke up when the ballplayers moved in. The diamond was in the center of town, right across the street from a pretty little yellow stucco house, home to the county jail. When the umpire called, "Play ball," the sheriff unlocked a cell and released a prisoner to keep score.

In '38, swing music was all the rage. The Sentimental Gentleman of Swing, Tommy Dorsey, was playing at Roseland. At converted speakeasies, renamed roadhouses, couples cut the rug doing the Lambeth walk. Town bands played in the parks on long summer nights, silver trombones flashing and the red eyes of Havana cigars winking in the fading light. *The Yearling* by Marjorie Kinnan Rawlings topped the bestseller list, and there were new novels by Edith Wharton, Virginia Woolf, and P. G. Wodehouse. But the book everyone was talking about was Daphne Du Maurier's *Rebecca*.

Such diversions were a momentary escape from the grim news of the day. In Europe an erstwhile housepainter was bullying his neighbors and threatening to march into Czechoslovakia unless Prague sliced off the Sudetenland. With memories of trench slaughter still fresh, the democracies were weakening. Britain's Neville Chamberlain was tiptoeing into talks with Hitler, prepared to cave in, sell out, concede, whatever was necessary to avert a second war. The Czechs were crying betrayal. Wars were raging around the globe. The civil war in Spain was in its third year. China and Japan were fighting in the Pacific, and in London's Bow Street Court, Countess Barbara Hutton Haugwitz-Reventlow was battling with her titled Danish husband for custody of their two-year-old son, Lance. The count was promising the beautiful five-and-dime-store heiress "three years of hell and headlines."

In America men peddled apples on streets that had once seemed paved with gold. FDR was in the White House, force-feeding the ailing nation an alphabet soup of relief programs. Martin Dies (D-Texas), chairman of the newly formed House

Un-American Activities Committee, was battling with Labor Secretary Frances Perkins to have Harry Bridges, president of the West Coast longshoremen's union, deported; New York's new mayor, Fiorello La Guardia, was trying to clean up after Tammany Hall's flamboyant Jimmy Walker. The Depression ground on. Soup lines were getting longer, and prosperity seemed as illusory as the kingdom of Oz, soon to be a major motion picture. Americans heard it all on the radio. Tuning in had become a new national pastime.

In homes across the country, the radio occupied a place of prominence. The big Philco console was a popular model — almost three feet of dark polished wood in an Art Deco design with gleaming dials. Like an honored guest, the radio was attended to closely but not understood fully. Families clustered around it, their attention fixed on its luminous face, imaginations drawing pictures to illustrate the words that came through the silvery mesh. Most listeners couldn't explain how the voice of a stranger, spoken from a great distance, came out of a polished box, but they accepted its validity on faith and never missed their favorite shows: *Amos 'n' Andy* and *The Green Hornet ("Faster, Kato, faster")*; the CBS News, with the young correspondents William Shirer and Edward R. Murrow reporting live from Berlin and London; and late in the evening, the remotes of the big bands — Duke Ellington, Benny Goodman, Artie Shaw, and Glenn Miller *("From the Pennsylvania Hotel's Café Rouge in New York City, Pennsylvania six, five 0-0-0")*.

Sunday evening was the most popular listening time. Living rooms filled with the voice of Lowell Thomas, dean of news commentators: *"Good evening, everybody. Today in Berlin, Nazi Germany staged a demonstration for its Führer as the rest of Europe tensely awaited a decision for war or peace."* On the radio, as in the movies, the news was a prelude to the featured attraction. Sunday nights, it was the *Chase and Sanborn Hour* on NBC at eight o'clock. For sixty minutes, storms of wind and war took a backseat to the banter of Edgar Bergen and Charlie McCarthy, prime-time radio's number one star.

When the comic and his smart-mouth dummy signed off at nine o'clock on the eighteenth of September, the storm that would become the Great Hurricane of 1938 was blowing on Florida's doorstep.

CHAPTER 3

A Shift in the Wind

When the first Neolithic man stepped out of the cave and looked up at the sky, he was attempting to predict the weather. We have been trying with varying degrees of success ever since. At the most fundamental level, weather is a cosmic balancing act. Because the earth is tilted on its axis, the sun doesn't warm it evenly. The most concentrated heat is at the equator, where the sun's rays are most direct; the least heat is at the poles.

Like a planetary central air conditioner, weather works to correct this inequity, shifting air so the tropics won't toast, the poles won't freeze, and we shall be spared a new ice age. Since the tropics are always hot and the poles are always cold, most of the unstable weather happens in the mid-latitudes. There, in the hospitable temperate zones, where the often frenetic pushing and shoving matches between warm and cold fronts occur, hurricanes and other epic weather dramas are played out.

———

In 1938, the first hint of trouble came early in September, when summer residents from Long Island to Cape Cod were closing up their beach houses, turning the water off to keep the pipes from bursting in winter and locking the doors for the first time all season. Halfway around the world at the Bilma oasis in the Sahara Desert, French meteorologists noticed a slight shift in the wind. An area of unstable air was passing over northwest Africa. Within a day or two, it had moved into the Atlantic around the Cape Verde Islands.

Every week or so, somewhere in the tropical seas off the northwest coast of Africa, a cluster of clouds comes together and takes on a sinister shape. Scattered thunderclouds tighten into a ring, and the winds within them begin to spiral. Only one out of every ten will intensify to hurricane force, and what makes one whorl of unstable air grow into a hurricane for every nine that peter out is as much conjecture as science. These incipient storms seem to be temperamental creatures, as sensitive to their surroundings as orchids, and they start to sputter unless atmospheric conditions are exactly right.

For a hurricane to form, the sea must be at least two hundred feet deep and the water surface more than 26° Celsius or about 80° degrees Fahrenheit. The cloud cluster must be close to the equator, but not too close. Five degrees north or south of the equatorial line and there's not enough planetary spin to create a cyclone. Thirty degrees north or south and there isn't enough humidity in the air to fuel the storm.

Given ideal conditions — warm, wet air; a revolving planet; uninterrupted sun-warmed seas; and no islands or volcanic mountains in the way to slow it down — and left to cruise across the Atlantic undisturbed, a cloud cluster may turn itself into a hurricane. The word derives from Huracán, the god of evil, whom the earliest Caribbean tribes feared above all other gods. The elements of wind and water were Huracán's weapons, and when he hurled them across the islands, the destruction was swift and absolute.

The French observation was beamed by shortwave radio to weather posts along the Caribbean Sea lanes. It clattered into the U.S. Weather Bureau station in Jacksonville, Florida, via Teletype, a vague threat amid a jumble of observations received from ships at sea and Caribbean port towns, from other U.S. weather posts, and from thousands of volunteer weather watchers across the country.

On September 4, the unstable air blowing from the Sahara gathered in the fertile Cape Verde breeding ground. Lying about four hundred miles west of Senegal in northwest Africa, the islands sit squarely in the path of the trade winds. Between them and the next landfall stretches a vast tropical incubator — two thousand miles of open, sun-warmed sea. So many North Atlantic hurricanes originate off Cape Verde that it is called "Hurricane Alley." The unstable air combined with moisture built up from the heat of the equator and formed a cluster of thunderclouds. The cloud cluster began to whirl. Floating nice and easy across the tropical seas, it pushed west on the Spanish Main, carried on the same powerful currents that brought Columbus from Europe to the New World. Lolling along at ten or twelve miles an hour, it covered 250 to 300 miles a day, drifting west at the same steady rate, encountering mile after mile of open water. With each mile, it grew stronger.

The spinning storm moved over warm tropical seas, where the air was humid and full of water vapor, the fuel that keeps a storm growing. As it swept across the ocean, gathering speed and strength, it blew the tops off waves, adding even more vapor to the air and more energy to its storehouse.

When surface winds reached twenty-five miles an hour, the system became a tropical depression. When they increased to fifty or sixty miles per hour, it became a tropical storm. When sustained winds reached seventy-four miles an hour, the storm reached the intensity of a tropical cyclone. A tropical cyclone has several names. In the Pacific Ocean it's called a typhoon. In the Philippines, a *baguio*. In the Tasman Sea, Australians call it a willy-willy. If it develops in the North Atlantic, it is called a hurricane.

At full strength, a tropical cyclone is an extreme low-pressure zone with more destructive might than the entire world arsenal. In one day it releases as much energy as the United States consumes in electric power in six months. If a way were ever found to harness one of these monster storms, the world's energy and water problems would be solved. No other force of nature can match its power, and nothing can stop it except another hurricane.

To understand its mechanics, imagine a toy top, one of those old-fashioned wooden ones with a string that wraps around it. Yank the string and the top takes off, spinning rapidly while simultaneously skidding across the floor. Now magnify that image millions of times. Like a top, a hurricane has two distinct movements — the rotation within and its forward push. The wind inside spirals around a central low-pressure axis, creating a tightly spinning whirlwind. The closer the wind is to the center, the faster it spins. The wind outside is an independent atmospheric force, pushing the disturbance forward in a specific direction and at a specific speed.

By the night of September 16, the random cloud cluster had traveled some fifteen hundred miles from Cape Verde to the Caribbean. Now a major cyclone, it was set on a collision course with Florida.

CHAPTER 4

Hurricane Watch

Friday, September 16

The hurricane watch began at the Jacksonville station of the U.S. Weather Bureau about suppertime on Friday, the sixteenth of September, when Grady Norton picked up a radio signal from a Brazilian freighter. The SS *Alegrete*, bound for her home port of Belém, had sailed into a cyclone in the Atlantic Ocean off the Leeward Islands. She reported pounding seas, seventy-five-mile-per-hour winds, and a barometric reading of 28.31 inches and falling.

If you were casting a hurricane hunter, a superhero battling the forces of wind, wave, and floodwater, Grady Norton would be an unlikely choice. A slight man of forty-three with thinning sandy hair, he was more Dagwood than Clark Kent. Norton combed his hair straight back, wore round oversize glasses, and in photographs often had a startled look. He had little formal education. His three favorite teachers were mythology, the Bible, and Shakespeare, and he quoted liberally from them to describe the weather he watched. Norton had worked in the U.S. Weather Bureau for almost twenty years, with time out for service in the

Army Signal Corps during World War I. In 1935 he was named director of the Weather Bureau's first hurricane center.

The original U.S. Weather Bureau was chartered by an act of Congress in 1870 and officially designated the Division of Telegrams and Reports for the Benefit of Commerce. As the name implies, it was devised as a tool for trade. A central Washington office, linked by telegram to a network of twenty-four observatories across the country, was set up to monitor the weather and issue daily forecasts. If storms, squalls, blizzards, frosts, and other Acts of God were predicted accurately, the thinking went, businesses could take protective measures and commerce would prosper. Within a few years, the agency had more than three hundred weather stations from coast to coast.

The Weather Bureau went through several configurations before Congress decided that a decentralized agency would respond more quickly to weather emergencies. In March 1935 the central office was replaced with forecasting stations strategically positioned in Washington, Jacksonville, New Orleans, and San Juan, Puerto Rico. The Jacksonville station was designated hurricane central, and Norton, a soft-spoken southerner from Choctaw County, Alabama, was transferred from New Orleans. He had been on the job for six months when the new system was tested for the first time. On Labor Day 1935, a Category 5 hurricane, the most intense tropical cyclone ever to strike the continental United States, hit the Florida Keys. Norton and his assistant, Gordon Dunn, saw it coming but misjudged its severity, and 428 people died.

Most of those killed were destitute World War I vets put to work by the New Deal building U.S. Highway 1. They died aboard the government train that was supposed to evacuate them. The rescue train did not reach the Keys until the height of the storm, and when it tried to return to the mainland, it was swept into the sea. In an article for *New Masses* magazine, Ernest Hemingway, one of the Keys' most celebrated residents, demanded to know "Who Murdered the Vets?" Gruesome reports of metal roofs that flew off shacks, guillotining the hapless men, and sheets of sand that sheared off their clothes, leaving nothing but belt buckles, horrified the nation. In the heart of the Great Depression, donations for a hurricane memorial poured in and a congressional committee convened to investigate what had gone so horribly wrong. Although the main culprit had been a paucity of information, Norton vowed to himself that not one more life would be lost to a hurricane on his watch. Now, almost three years to the day later, another killer storm was blowing toward Florida and the same two-man team would track it.

A weather forecaster who does not own a raincoat, hat, or umbrella is either supremely optimistic or supremely confident. Gordon Dunn, Jacksonville's assistant director of hurricane forecasting, was probably a bit of both. When his predictions were off, he would arrive at the station dripping wet and dry off as he worked. Cool and resourceful, Dunn had earned a reputation as one of the best mappers in the Bureau. He was about ten years younger than Norton, taller and broad-shouldered, with a craggy handsomeness. Both men were farm boys — Norton grew up on an Alabama dirt farm, Dunn on a Vermont dairy farm — and both had a dry humor. In most other ways, they were poles apart.

Norton was folksy, Dunn was reserved. Norton, intuitive; Dunn, analytical. Norton trusted empirical observations; Dunn was a stickler for mathematical precision. Dunn loved to squaredance; Norton had two left feet. Dunn would write the definitive book on Atlantic hurricanes. Norton avoided putting much in writing. He believed that you never track the same storm twice.

Their different approaches reflected the changing state of meteorology in 1938. However individual their styles, though, on the Friday night of September 16, 1938, the two men were in accord. With another killer storm in their sights, they were not taking any chances.

In the thirties, without sophisticated tools to guide them, forecasters relied almost entirely on surface observations. Data came in to the Weather Bureau continuously from shortwave radio transmitters and a Teletype network linked to every major port in the Caribbean. As they received additional information, Norton and Dunn located the storm within the Caribbean and within the context of the prevailing atmospheric conditions. According to their best estimates, it was sauntering at twenty miles an hour due east, and within the system, cyclonic winds were whirling at 109 miles an hour.

Until Benjamin Franklin picked up a Boston newspaper one day in 1743, storms were assumed stationary, having no forward motion. Franklin read about a storm in Boston and realized that the same rains had visited Philadelphia the night before, spoiling his plans to observe a lunar eclipse. From this he deduced that storms could travel great distances. Nine hundred miles of warm open water — the nourishment that hurricanes thrive on — separated this storm from Miami. It was centered about 450 miles north of San Juan and east of the Bahamas. Barring any change in direction, it would hit the Bahamas Monday night and drive straight into Dade County sometime on Tuesday, September 20.

Saturday, September 17

On Saturday morning Floridians woke up to the sound of Grady Norton's easy drawl: "A tropical disturbance of dangerous proportions is gathering in the Caribbean. Traveling at twenty miles per hour in an easterly direction, it should reach the Miami-Dade area sometime Tuesday morning. Every precaution should be taken in the face of this dangerous storm."

As the hurricane developed, Norton issued so many weather updates, he became known across the state as Mr. Hurricane, his voice as familiar in Florida as Arthur Godfrey's broadcasting from the pink mirage of Miami's Roney Plaza. Norton's report was the first statewide storm warning ever broadcast in Florida. Twenty-five stations carried the alert, and from the Keys to Miami's Collins Avenue the response was immediate and intense.

Remembering Labor Day 1935, anxious residents began barricading their homes and businesses, dry-docking their boats, clearing out of the path of the storm. The Red Cross called up extra relief workers, pulling them from New York and New England and dispatching them to Florida. The Coast Guard sent radio trucks to outlying areas of the state. WPA (Work Projects Administration) and CCC (Civilian Conservation Corps) workers received immediate orders to begin evacuating camps in the Keys. Miami newspapers reprinted photographs of the ghastly devastation of '35 under headlines that asked IS IT HAPPENING AGAIN?

Norton and Dunn were determined the answer would be no. During hurricane season, from June to November, they routinely alternated twenty-four-hour shifts and issued weather updates every six hours, seven days a week. Now, with a dangerous cyclone in their sights, they set up a surplus army cot in a corner of the station and remained on duty around the clock. They would monitor the approaching hurricane continuously for more than one hundred hours, from Friday evening, September 16, to the early-morning hours of Wednesday, September 21.

———

In 1686, before he had sighted the comet that bears his name, Edmond Halley drew and published the first weather map. But it was not until Marconi invented the wireless telegraph some two hundred years later that maps became an essential weather tool. Marconi's invention revolutionized forecasting, transforming meteorology from an empirical art to a science.

With the invention of the telegraph, ships at sea could communicate directly with weather stations. The first ship-to-shore report was transmitted on December 3, 1905, and the first wireless hurricane communiqué came four years later, when the SS *Cartago* ran into a tropical cyclone off the coast of Yucatán.

Direct and immediate communication allowed forecasters to translate the observations they received into same-day, even same-hour, charts called synoptic maps. Often described as weather snapshots, synoptic maps give a picture, or a series of pictures, of atmospheric conditions — barometric pressure, temperature, humidity, precipitation, winds, and cloud cover — over a broad area at a specific point in time.

Whether hand-drawn as they were in the 1930s or computer-generated as they are today, synoptic maps are critical to forecasting, especially the map showing barometric pressure. Barometric pressure levels are the clearest measure of a hurricane's strength. A precipitous drop means a storm is intensifying. Any rise indicates a weakening. On a barometric map, lines, called isobars, are drawn to link points of equal pressure. The density of isobars indicates the strength and location of a storm.

During their hurricane watch, Norton and Dunn continually drew new maps. By comparing successive charts, they could see how weather systems were moving and evolving over a broad area at a specific time. Maps drawn with speed and skill were the key to an accurate prediction, and Dunn was a master of synoptic mapping. According to his seven o'clock reckoning, on Saturday night the storm was thirty miles closer to Miami, moving at approximately the same speed and still on course. With low-pressure, tightly packed isobars spelling a serious hurricane, a statewide emergency was declared. Throughout the day and night, Jacksonville telegraphed constant updates to newspaper offices and radio stations nationwide. In spite of their urgency, few beyond the panhandle took note.

Disasters always seemed to happen in far-off places with romantic names, and in September, Florida was still a season away. In 1938 attention didn't usually turn south until blizzards were blanketing New England.

Sunday, September 18

The storm intensified through the night. By two o'clock Sunday afternoon, winds were blowing at 150 miles per hour. Strong shifting squalls enveloped the Caribbean islands from Puerto Rico to the Bahamas. Coconut palms bent into the gale, rains blasted flimsy shelters, and winds shrieked like banshees over a tremendous, raging sea. The hurricane continued to deepen through the night. By two A.M. Monday, it was a Category 5 storm.

The official gauge of a hurricane's destructive force is the Saffir-Simpson Damage Potential Scale. Storms are measured according to sustained wind speed, storm surge height, and barometric pressure and classified on a scale of 1 to 5, 5 being "catastrophic." Only one Category 5 storm had ever reached the continental United States — Labor Day 1935. The Labor Day hurricane had been a tightly coiled tropical cyclone — small, swift, and singularly nasty. The Hurricane of 1938 was shaping up to be a big, sprawling mother storm — some five hundred miles in diameter, as big as the state of Ohio.

Although Galileo proved long ago that man is not the center of the universe, we tend to take weather personally. If it rains, it is raining on our parade. If it shines, it is shining for our benefit. Most days we go along blithely unconcerned that directly over our heads is a vast, never static sea of gases that we can't control and only partially understand. That gaseous ocean is immense and mysterious, yet we largely ignore it until weather as formidable as an extreme hurricane strikes and we face a force infinitely mightier and more savage than ourselves.

Monday, September 19

With a catastrophic Category 5 hurricane poised to strike Miami–Palm Beach, the rest of the country finally glanced south. The *New York Times* ran a front-page story, HURRICANE IN ATLANTIC HEADS TOWARD FLORIDA, warning that the Weather Bureau was expecting "a storm of dangerous proportions." Newspapers in New England printed the alarm as well.

At eight o'clock Monday morning, daylight saving time, the hurricane was about 650 miles east-southeast of Florida, centered at latitude 23° north, longitude 70° west, and moving at twenty miles an hour. If it maintained a constant speed and direction, it would pass through the Bahamas overnight, spreading gales and squalls over a wide area. Winds would pick up along the Florida coast, and Miami would wake up with the hurricane on its doorstep. At 10:30 A.M. Jacksonville issued a clear warning: *Florida's east coast is in the danger zone of this storm and all interests are urged to stand by for possible hurricane warnings during the day.*

Though not the mangrove swamp it had been before the land rush of the 1920s, Miami in the thirties was a far cry from its later Gold Coast years. The heyday of Lincoln Road and Collins Avenue would not arrive until after the war, and the big push of luxury hotels and motel strips would not happen until the fifties. Except for the extravagant Roney Plaza, the sands north of the famous crossroads were mostly barren. Sportsmen went to the Keys for the deep-sea fishing, and gamblers and high rollers headed to Havana. The southern terminus of wealth was Palm Beach.

On a good day in 1938, Miami felt like a town frozen in time. The city had woken up from the grandiose dream of the winter playland pioneered by entrepreneur Carl Fisher and railroad tycoon Henry Morrison Flagler. In its place was the bleak reality of the Great Depression. Homes and office buildings begun before the crash stood unfinished. Streets laid out in the land grab of the twenties defined empty neighborhoods.

Miami had been on full alert throughout the weekend, and by Monday morning the city looked like a frontier film set on a Hollywood back lot. The pastel town was a drab fortress brown. Stucco and glass facades were wrapped in protective timber. Billboards had been taken down, dangling street signs removed. The Red Cross had turned police stations and schools into emergency shelters, bringing in cots and setting up first-aid stations. Dry-goods stores were doing a land-office business. There was a run on candles, flashlights, batteries, and kerosene lamps. Grocery store shelves were suddenly bare. Floridians stocked up on food and ordered extra ice blocks for their iceboxes. At home they filled every spare receptacle with water — stockpots, pitchers, barrels, buckets, jugs, sinks, and bathtubs.

———

Waiting and watching as a hurricane approaches land is tantamount to playing the seventh game of the World Series. Everything is on the line. Except to wash and change their clothes, Grady Norton and Gordon Dunn had not left the weather station since Friday. Every detail, every decision, what they did and what they failed to do would be critical. The two men were at the breaking point. "By the time you wrestle with one of these big blows for a couple of days without letup, you're about ready for a padded cell," Norton would say.

Gordon Dunn would second that. He called the typical Cape Verde hurricane "a schizophrenic sort of creature." Although it is a phenomenon of warm water, it always blows away from the tropics and at the first opportunity moves northward toward the colder water that will destroy it. Once it crosses the Caribbean, it usually recurves, veering north-northeast, and goes out to sea before reaching the continental United States. It is steered on this course by the currents of the Bermuda High, a mass of dense dry air that dominates the weather in the North Atlantic over many miles.

Most hurricanes originating in Cape Verde follow this predictable, and suicidal, course. They come across the Caribbean, loop around the Bermuda High, and dissipate in the busy shipping lanes between the United States and Europe. Before they curve, hurricanes signal their intention by slowing down. But this Category 5 behemoth was not following the pattern. Instead of diminishing, it was accelerating. In twenty-four hours it traveled almost six hundred miles on the same direct path toward Biscayne Bay. Norton and Dunn were tracking it with extreme caution, questioning, analyzing, and weighing every possibility. Was this ferocious Category 5 hurricane a typical Cape Verde blow, or was it a freak that would defy the conventional track? Would it make the classic turn and follow the predictable path out to sea, or hold its present course, as they feared, and barrel into Florida?

At two o'clock Monday afternoon, the storm was still on track and advancing rapidly. Norton broadcast an urgent alarm: *All interests in southern Florida should immediately make all possible preliminary preparations to withstand this severe storm and then stand by for later advisories. Hurricane warnings will probably be issued tonight.*

As the afternoon lengthened, the air in the station grew as stale as a half-eaten sandwich. Doors and windows were open wide. The heat was cloying. The crackle of radios mixed with the whir of the overhead fan, the buzz of flies, the incessant *chit-chit-chit* of the Teletype machines, and the constant ringing of the telephone. Dunn was stretched out on the army cot, trying to cat-nap and failing miserably. Norton fielded calls from anxious relief workers and jittery officials in Washington and Tampa, seeking assurance that there would be no Labor Day sequel. Reporters hung around the station, hoping for an interview or at least a good quote.

Because forecasting is such a dicey business even today, frustrations build, and every so often a preemptive strike is launched to weaken or "seed" a storm before it comes ashore. The argument for seeding is straightforward: take out the monster before it can do any damage. Efforts, from the clever to the bizarre, have included seeding a hurricane with dry ice (Project Cirrus) or silver iodide crystals (Project Stormfury), spreading plastic sheets across the sea, detonating a nuclear device within the eye of the storm, even bombarding the eye with tons of ice cubes. None has ever succeeded.

In Jacksonville every precaution short of seeding had been taken. Evacuation plans were complete. Emergency services were in place. Everyone was restless and on edge. Only the alligators in the Everglades were snoozing calmly. Animals are always the first to sense a disturbance in the weather. The approach of a storm makes them snarling and surly, like bad drunks, and in fact, a hurricane actually has an intoxicating effect. The lowered atmospheric pressure reduces the oxygen level in the blood, just as alcohol does. As the sun dropped on Monday night, the alligators in the Florida Everglades were a picture of tranquillity.

Hurricanes are supple tricksters. For reasons scientists still cannot explain, just when a forecaster thinks he has their number, they gull him with an unexpected zig or zag that sets them on a different course. In an instant, placid waters rampage and dangerous seas becalm. Through the early evening, observations began to trickle in to Jacksonville suggesting that the extreme hurricane might be veering. It had zipped passed Haiti and was skirting the Bahamas. The barometer was falling more slowly in the outer islands, and winds were shifting. Weather stations in Havana signaled that the storm would not touch Cuba.

Hunched over his desk, Dunn began to redraw the maps. As the features of the new charts emerged, they seemed to suggest that the storm would hook sharply north-northeast and follow the typical path of a Cape Verde blow. Still, he and Norton were reluctant to take any chances with such a tricky system. They decided to maintain storm warnings from Key West to Jacksonville while issuing a tentative statewide all clear: *Danger from a tropical hurricane would seem to be past, but caution is advised for the next twelve hours.*

As the hurricane continued to curve, they became cautiously optimistic. Their 7:30 P.M. bulletin advised: *Interests on the southeast Florida coast are urged not to relax their vigilance until the re-curving tendency is definitely established.* By ten o'clock Monday night, the eye of the storm was about 360 miles east of Palm Beach and still veering north. Ship-to-shore messages confirmed the altered trajectory. Jacksonville radioed an all-clear advisory for the Miami area.

Tuesday, September 20

Although it was still a storm "of great intensity," the Great Hurricane of 1938 appeared to be set on the classic route to oblivion. The barometer was creeping up one-sixteenth of an inch and winds were slowing. Estimating that the center would pass some distance east of the Carolina capes, the Jacksonville team ordered storm warnings along the North Carolina coast between Wilmington and Cape Hatteras, and cautioned mariners: *All vessels in path and all small craft from the Virginia Capes to Charleston should remain in harbor until the storm passes.*

By eight o'clock Tuesday night it was still curving north-northeast. Winds had diminished to 138 miles an hour from a morning high of 155. The Category 5 storm was downgraded to a Category 3. Grady Norton sent Dunn home. He expected the storm to lose steam in the colder northern waters and flatten out in the busy shipping routes of the North Atlantic. At worst, it might cause a few cases of seasickness. At about 10:30 P.M. he broadcast a confident message: *The storm may come close enough to cause strong winds but I feel safe in saying there will be no hurricane winds for Florida.*

If it kept to its new northeastern path, the storm would continue to brush by the Bahamas, swing up the coast, and knock itself out at sea without ever touching land. Good news for Florida, but tricky for ships at sea.

Although he did not expect any surprises, Norton maintained his hurricane watch, tracking the storm through Tuesday night. It continued to advance at a steady twenty miles per hour, until Wednesday morning. At about two o'clock on September 21, it began to accelerate. Doubling its speed to forty miles an hour, it sprinted up the coast. This was the first sign that the Great Hurricane of 1938 would not follow the rules.

CHAPTER 5

At Sea

On Tuesday night, September 20, the SS *Conte di Savoia* was steaming toward New York. The Italian liner was due to arrive the following evening, four hours after the RMS *Queen Mary* departed for her return trip to Southampton. The two ships should pass in the night.

The *Conte di Savoia* was smaller than most of the grand liners — 814 feet long and just under forty-nine tons. Fitted out in rococo splendor, she and her sister ship, the *Rex*, were the pride of the Italian line. The *Conte*'s grand Colonna Lounge was girded with marble columns, and statues were poised on pedestals beneath a frescoed ceiling. The gracious service and superb kitchen matched her lavish appointments. On the menu were the finest Parma prosciutto, feather-light gnocchi tossed in a subtle walnut sauce, veal chops stuffed with pâté de foie gras, and risotto with white truffles. Her urbane captain, Alberto Ottino, took personal pride in each dish served.

A veteran of many transatlantic crossings and a man of keen enthusiasms, Ottino strode the deck as if it were a stage. A ship's captain must be an actor as well as a sailor, performing for the pleasure of his passengers. On this voyage he was carrying two thousand. One of the passengers was Ernesto Gherzi, a Jesuit priest and meteorologist.

In the early 1900s Jesuits were regarded as near-mystical hurricane hunters. Armed with their own empirical observations and only the most basic tools — a sextant, barometer, and anemometer to measure wind velocity — Jesuits stationed in Cuba, the Philippines, and Shanghai forecast the arrival of tropical cyclones with almost preternatural accuracy. Father Gherzi had spent twenty-three years at the Zi-ka-wei weather observatory in Shanghai. Built by the Jesuits in the 1900s, Zi-ka-wei was the most important meteorological station in Asia. During his years there, Father Gherzi had made a special study of typhoons. "On the China coast we have twenty, thirty, forty typhoons a year," he liked to say. "After a while you can forget your instruments and just sniff one coming."

The Jesuit was a Savonarola of the sea. His forecasts were so uncannily accurate, the Chinese named him "typhoon father." But the Boxer Rebellion put an end to his work. Many of the Jesuits were massacred. Father Gherzi was lucky to escape with his life. Now the official weather forecaster for the Italian airline and shipping company, he was sailing to the United States to visit meteorological institutes and weather stations. He planned to stay at Georgetown University and tour the Naval Observatory, the Bureau of Standards, and the D.C. Weather Bureau.

The *Conte di Savoia* had departed from Genoa on September 14, making stops at Naples, Cannes, and Gibraltar before beginning the transatlantic crossing. On the morning of Sunday, the eighteenth, while she was skimming along on an uneventful sea, Father Gherzi had warned the captain: "One of my children will be visiting soon." Captain Ottino dismissed his caution as Jesuitical mumbo-jumbo, pointing out that there was not so much as a whitecap on the ocean. He joked that he would throw the typhoon father overboard if he made any more dire pronouncements.

By the night of the twentieth, the *Conte di Savoia* was thirty-six hours from New York Harbor. The captain, who had a sweet, lyric voice that he liked to think had echoes of the popular tenor Beniamino Gigli, was entertaining a group of first-class passengers with "Che Gelida Manina" from *La Bohème* when a radioman brought him the hurricane caution. If Jacksonville's calculations were correct, the *Conte di Savoia* would sail directly into the extreme hurricane. Captain Ottino read the message and turned salt white. The priest's words came back to him like a prophecy. He rushed up to the bridge, shouting for the Jesuit. Now, according to the Americans, the hurricane the priest had prophesized was approaching rapidly.

Father Gherzi stood watch, as he had done through most of the voyage, in apparent communion with the sea. It was Bible black now, silent and satiny. Black cassock flapping against spindle legs, long, slender fingers clamped on his broad-brimmed *cappello*, he looked like a strange crow perched on the bridge. Father Gherzi was about six foot four and reed-thin with close-cropped graying hair and a Vandyke beard. He conversed in Latin, Italian, Mandarin Chinese, and half a dozen other languages with equal ease and possessed a calm containment that quieted the captain's alarm.

When Ottino repeated the radio message, the Jesuit shrugged. "I think the weather gods knew I was coming to the eastern coast and sent the typhoon with me." Father Gherzi stayed on the bridge for several more hours, watching the sea, studying the cloud formations, and listening to the wind. Then he assured the captain that there was nothing more to fear. The *Conte di Savoia* would skirt the storm, not sail into it, as the U.S. Weather Bureau was predicting. Although she might encounter squalls from the outer edge of the disturbance, Ottino did not have to reduce speed or alter course. The hurricane was moving north too fast for the paths of ship and storm to converge.

This time Captain Ottino heeded the "typhoon father's" forecast and held his ship on course. The *Conte di Savoia* would slip into New York Harbor just after the hurricane had blown through.

Six hundred vacationers had booked the Cunard–White Star Line's Caribbean cruise. They sailed from the Hudson River pier on Saturday, September 17, paying from $122.50 for a thirteen-day trip to Kingston, Havana, and Nassau. Billed as "the finest of Cunarders," the RMS *Carinthia* was built to be a floating pleasure palace. Among the amenities were instantaneous hot running water in every stateroom, beds six inches wider than on other ships, racquet courts, a full gym with sundeck, two promenade decks, two sea-view lounges, indoor and outdoor swimming pools, a movie theater, a cardroom, and a cocktail deck. Even the second-class public rooms were paneled to evoke the feel of a British country house. Once renowned for her luxurious round-the-world voyages, by 1938 the aging vessel was reduced to Caribbean cruises. The leisurely jaunts of eight to thirteen days offered first-run movies, dance classes, and two orchestras.

Captaining the *Carinthia* was A. C. Greig, an Aussie with a crisp no-nonsense manner. Greig had the compact, boxy body of a Morris Minor, a chin as cleft as Cary Grant's, and an affinity for the composer whose name he almost shared. The *Peer Gynt Suite* was a standard in the repertoire of the ship's orchestras. Greig was a cautious captain, and throughout the weekend as the *Carinthia* glided south, he maintained a constant watch on the hurricane that was heading toward Florida. Greig was concerned for his passengers' comfort. They had not booked passage for a harrowing maritime adventure. They wanted a relaxing cruise — midnight suppers of cold lobster and champagne, carefree lessons learning the Lindy in the arms of flattering young hoofers. Broadway hopefuls hungry for work signed on cruise ships as stewards, harboring a fantasy that they might be glimpsed by one of the Tin Pan Alley legends — Cole Porter, say, or Richard Rodgers — who regularly booked passage on the Cunard liners.

Tuesday morning the *Carinthia* was about 150 miles north of Florida, and the Weather Bureau was still expecting the storm to hit Miami later in the day. To play it safe and assure his passengers a smooth sailing, the captain adjusted his course, bearing west to hug the southern coast and put more than a hundred miles between the *Carinthia* and the storm. Through the day, barometric pressure held steady at 29.71, indicating stable weather. Greig, a crisp, assured commander, was confident that he had steered his ship clear of danger. But late in the afternoon, the sky turned slate gray, and sundown brought an unnatural calm. It stilled the offshore waters and aggravated Greig's worries, giving him a sour stomach. Instead of turning out of the path of the killer cyclone, as the hurricane recurved, the *Carinthia* was sailing into it.

By ten P.M., winds were humming past the glass-enclosed decks. Rain burst from above as if it had broken through a solid ceiling. As the ship lurched into the tumult, chandeliers swung like church bells and dangling crystal prisms clinked like glasses raised in a final toast. Fox-trotting couples careened across the dance floor and tumbled into the orchestra. Tables slid after them, and trays of cocktails crashed to the floor, the tinkle of breaking glass barely perceptible over the storm's insistent voice.

Hurricane winds blew the tops off the tremendous sea. Waves rushed the ship from all sides, falling on her decks with crushing force. Clipped onto safety lines, their oilskins plastered against them like second skins, the crew cleared the decks, roped off promenades, covered portholes, lashed down lifeboats. In the first furious squall, the sea hissed like a thousand snakes.

The captain ordered the orchestra to play louder and faster, a frenzy of gaiety to drown out the din — "A-tisket, a-tasket / A green and yellow basket." And he ordered the champagne to flow, even when chilled silver buckets became receptacles for not-so-genteel heaving and chucking. Stewards slipped on steps slick with vomit. Passengers who had retired for an early sleep or to return to the sinister goings-on at Manderley were jarred into wakefulness by the ocean banging against the portholes and tossed out of their berths.

One of the Cunard Line's magnificent new *Queen*s might have been heavy enough to weather such an epic storm, but the *Carinthia* was a smaller ship. Her intimate size, opulent appointments, and gleaming white paint suggested an oversize yacht. When she and her sister ship, the *Franconia*, were launched in the twenties, they had inaugurated a new breed of sea vessels — the one-stackers, smaller, 20,000-ton ships (624 feet long by 73 feet wide) designed for luxury.

The *Carinthia* took the hurricane head-on. She plunged into the trough of the sea, slamming against it as if she were running into a cement wall, then staggered out, only to nose-dive again. Great swells rolled her down. The deck filled with white water as though heaped with snow. The ocean brawled, the wind bayed, and the old ship bowed to them, tumbling into the sea, struggling out, tumbling in again. She was helpless before the beating.

In the West Indies sailors divide a hurricane into two semicircles, one navigable, the other deadly. Although the *Carinthia* was on the navigable western side on Tuesday night, alone in a hurling and horrible sea, the distinction seemed moot. Greig's options were few and generally futile. If he lowered the lifeboats, they would be lost instantly. A Mayday message would be a cry in the wilderness. If there were other ships in the vicinity, they would be fighting for their own survival. Like sea captains from Noah to Ahab, Greig had to battle the devil alone. For the first time in his long years at sea, he thought of his ship as a casket.

The wind swept at him out of a vast obscurity. He felt the *Carinthia* shudder as if her very boards and bolts were aching; he heard the groan of metal against metal. The bottom fell out of the barometer. The *Carinthia* was taking aboard huge quantities of rain and seawater. The crew pumped continuously through the night to keep the holds from flooding. Bilge pumps strained to the breaking point. The ship's lights flickered, dimmed, flickered again. Stokers fed the furnace like men possessed to keep her going. Muscles cramped with the effort. If power was lost, the *Carinthia* would be so much flotsam at the mercy of the merciless sea. If the steering gear held and the engines turned, if the decks did not splinter under the weight of the water, and the bow was not buried when the ship stumbled into a monster swell, then there was hope that she would ride out the storm.

About three o'clock Wednesday morning, the *Carinthia* staggered free of the hurricane zone. The stunned captain radioed to shore that the barometer had dropped almost an inch to 27.85 in less than an hour. It was one of the lowest readings ever recorded in the North Atlantic.

Today the National Hurricane Center (NHC) is a meteorological CIA, detecting and stalking nature's terrorists. At its headquarters in Dade County, Florida, the NHC maintains a continuous watch on the waters of the Atlantic from May 15 through September 30. Weather satellites orbit the equator; others fly from pole to pole. A Doppler radar network extends from the Gulf of Mexico to southern Canada. "Hurricane hunters" — Air Force WC-130 Hercules planes — fly reconnaissance missions into and around tropical cyclones. During critical periods when a hurricane is building, round-the-clock shifts maintain a constant watch on the system. Fleets of Gulfstream IV jets and P-3 Orion turboprops also gather data. Man and machine interpret the torrent of meteorological intelligence. Mathematical computer models of the hurricane are used to analyze the information, relate it to prevailing weather patterns, and compare it with the documented hurricanes of history.

As a dangerous system moves into the Caribbean or the Gulf of Mexico, the NHC makes hourly reconnaissance flights. Residents in potential danger zones are put on guard. Relief agencies are alerted. A twenty-four-hour weather channel provides regular updates of the advancing storm. But tropical storms remain so unpredictable that forecasts are only accurate within twenty-four hours of landfall.

In 1938 the U.S. Weather Bureau was a chain of relay bases located at key points along the coast. Each station monitored storms in its region. Jacksonville would track a hurricane as far north as Carolina's Outer Banks. When the storm reached Cape Hatteras, the D.C. office took over and issued forecasts for the northern half of the Atlantic seaboard. Forecasting tools were equally primitive. Weather balloons and aerial reconnaissance were in the experimental stage, and radar was the stuff that Norton and Dunn must have dreamed about on all-clear days when no storm front loomed.

"Whenever I have a difficult challenge in deciding and planning where and when to issue hurricane warnings," Norton said,

"I usually stroll out of the office onto the roof, put my foot on the parapet ledge, look out over the Everglades, and say a little prayer."

About four A.M. on Wednesday, September 21, Norton's prayer was answered. The storm had swept by Florida and was whistling up the coast. The hurricane watch in Jacksonville officially ended. As the storm headed for the Carolina capes, responsibility for tracking passed to the Washington station. Exhausted after monitoring the blow for more than one hundred hours, Grady Norton signed off with a final advisory to "ships in the path of this severe storm."

His caution was heeded too well. Storm warnings were hoisted along the shore, all the way to Eastport, Maine, and ships that otherwise would have reported from the danger zone either stayed in port or headed for the open ocean.

On Wednesday, September 21, 1938, there would be few ship-to-shore observations, and the man in D.C. assigned to track the storm would be Charles Pierce, a junior forecaster who had never encountered a full-blown hurricane before. At the age of twenty-seven, Pierce would experience a singular baptism by fire — a sudden and complete immersion into one of the most intense and deadliest hurricanes ever to come ashore in the continental United States.

CHAPTER 6

All Aboard

On Wednesday, September 21, 1938, Katharine Hepburn woke up with the sun at her family's summer house in Fenwick, Connecticut. Located at the point where the mouth of the Connecticut River and Long Island Sound meet, Fenwick was a company getaway for Aetna Life Insurance of Hartford, about forty-five miles north. Like Napatree–Watch Hill, just across the state border, it was exclusively a summer colony, and by mid-September almost everything in town was locked, shuttered, and stored away for another season. In the rambling Victorian houses with their broad verandas and clear ocean views, beds were stripped and furniture was covered with old sheets.

The Hepburns' house was one of the few still open. Dick Hepburn, an aspiring playwright, had stayed on after Labor Day, trying to finish his new play, a caustic romantic comedy about a willful, uppity actress and her socially inept millionaire boyfriend. Any resemblance to persons living or dead, including his sister and Howard Hughes, he insisted, was purely coincidental. Kate stayed on, too, her life pretty much up in the air. She was waiting for the final word on Scarlett, waiting for the final draft of Philip Barry's new play, *The Philadelphia Story*, waiting for a phone call from Howard. Their romance was on hold. Hughes's picture had been showing up every other day in some magazine or newspaper, usually with Bette Davis or Ginger Rogers, Hollywood's highest-paid stars, on his arm. It rankled, especially since their salaries were twice what she had ever made. Hepburn's image as *the* independent woman was mostly myth, a Hollywood fantasy that she cultivated. Throughout her life, she was always dependent on a strong man.

But this Wednesday Kate woke up feeling as fine as the morning. She had finally called Howard the night before, not to give him an answer to his marriage proposal but to ask for advice. Their romance might be in limbo, complicated in no small part by her parents' disapproval, but there was no one she trusted more. Hughes had bolstered her floundering career, buying the rights to *Bringing Up Baby* when RKO shelved it. He was releasing the film himself at the end of the year. Now, she told him, *The Philadelphia Story* was headed for Broadway, and she had agreed to play Tracy Lord, with one reservation — "provided I don't play Scarlett O'Hara first."

Hughes listened. Then he gave his girl the advice that would eventually bring her back to the West Coast and make her one of Hollywood's biggest and wealthiest stars: "Buy the film rights before you open, kiddo." His check to cover the cost was in the mail.

So Wednesday morning Hepburn greeted the appearance of the sun with more than her usual gusto. The tide was low, a light breeze was on the air, and her life was looking brighter than it had in weeks. She went for a bracing eight A.M. swim, then dashed off to the fairway to play nine holes of golf. A light sea breeze was stirring when she reached the Fenwick Golf Club.

Hepburn piled her red hair in a bun to keep it from flying in her eyes and teed off. The breeze quickened with each hole she played. On the par three ninth, she set herself and swung. The strong, high drive caught the wind. The ball sailed, sailed, sailed, and dropped into the ninth hole. Her first hole in one! It gave her a score of thirty-one on the nine holes, her best game ever. Pleased as punch, she decided to go for a second swim after lunch. The wind was sharpening across the Northeast Corridor, bringing with it the best surf of the summer.

That same morning at eleven o'clock in New York, City, the boarding call echoed in the cavernous halls of Grand Central Terminal, emptying the oak benches in the Forty-second Street waiting room. Passengers streamed across the station beneath the vaulted ceiling traced with the constellations, past the circular marble information booth where the stationmaster was writing "on time" on the black glass board beside the name *Bostonian*, onto the platform where the silver train was belching steam.

First-class passengers hurried down the platform to the Oriental, the posh parlor car at the end of the train. Each seat was a cushiony armchair with white linen antimacassars on the arms and back. The chairs swiveled 360 degrees, and beside each was a button to ring for the steward, who would bring drinks to the seats. The other passengers crowded onto the coaches. Many were students going back to prep schools and colleges in New England for the start of the new school year.

A redcap, his dolly piled with luggage, escorted seventeen-year-old Elvine Richard and her mother to a rear coach. Elvine was on her way to boarding school in Massachusetts. Roderick Hagenbuckle, a young teacher at the Fessenden School just outside Boston, was shepherding twenty-five boys, ages fourteen to seventeen, to Back Bay Station. Their new blue suits, from Brooks Brothers or Best & Co., looked stiff and a little too big, but the boys would grow into them, or out of them, by the end of the term. Lawrence Burwell was going to Providence for his senior year at Brown University. Ed Flanagan and his wife also had tickets to Providence. Flanagan was the chairman of the Democratic City Committee there.

The crack New York–Boston Shore Line Limited filled up quickly. Joe Richards, the conductor, checked his gold pocket watch, called a final "All aboard," and swung onto the train. At eleven o'clock, exactly on schedule, the *Bostonian* departed from Grand Central, carrying 275 passengers and making stops at 125th Street; New Haven; Old Saybrook; New London; Mystic; Stonington; Westerly, Rhode Island; North Kingston; Providence; and Back Bay Station, Boston.

At approximately 11:30 A.M., out on the rocks at Weekapaug, Rhode Island, a couple of miles east of Watch Hill, Mrs. John McKesson Camp eyed the sky uncertainly. She was a woman who knew her own mind and had no compunctions about letting others know it, too. But now she was wavering: should she fold up the tablecloth and send her picnic guests home, or open the wicker hamper? The surf was breaking high on the rocks, showering spumes of spray on her picnic site. Very strange, indeed. The tide shouldn't peak for hours, yet it seemed to be coming in rapidly. Highly peculiar, but then it had been a peculiar season.

On nearby Napatree, the postman was making his daily rounds. He knocked on the glassed-in front porch where Jessie Moore and her daughter, Havila (no relation to their neighbors, the Geoffrey Moores) had front-row seats to the weather spectacle. The Moores had been summering at Napatree for years.

Havila, forty and crippled since birth, could float freely in the surf in front of their cottage. Although her husband was arriving for the weekend, Mrs. Moore gave the mailman a letter for him:

> *Watch Hill, Wednesday — 6:30 A.M.*
>
> *Dear Fred,*
>
> *Never stopped raining since you left. Some beautiful ocean raging. Surf high coming over wall. Plenty of wind from southwest. It is not cold at all. We are getting along fine and I love to look at the ocean. Havila preparing to go home. Am packing.*
>
> Love, Jessie
>
> *Just out looking at water. High tide 6:30. Just turning and each wave comes almost on front porch. You could get plenty of fine planks if here. Fine steps just floated near our step.*

A few houses away, Catherine Moore glanced out her bedroom window just in time to see her son, Geoffrey, flying down the bay. A southeast wind was whipping his sister Anne's sailboat at a good clip out toward the end of Napatree Point, with Geoffrey in hot pursuit. Beyond the point lay the open Atlantic, not the safest place for a boy in a rowboat with a stiff breeze at his back. He would never be able to row back against the wind. Catherine called the Coast Guard.

She had hoped for an uneventful day. There was so much to do. The laundry had piled up and she wanted to get it on the line while the sun was shining. Geoffrey was going to prep school at the end of the week — she had to finish labeling and packing his clothes. Then there was the house — they would be closing it for the season, with all that entailed.

Catherine watched until she spotted a Coast Guard boat setting out. Feeling easier, she went down to the laundry room to help her cook, Loretta. Once the clothes were snapping on the line, double-pinned because a breeze was picking up, Catherine returned to the bedroom window with her husband Jeff's binoculars and trained them on Little Narragansett Bay. The water, which on most days was as glassy as a skating rink, was choppy. She scanned the shoreline all the way to the tip.

There were a dozen or so swimmers on the bay side, and the boys out on the water, still scooting along, having too much fun to worry about getting back. The ocean side was almost deserted. She picked out two men — fishermen, probably, or clammers — and just beyond them a couple. She smiled to herself. *Frolicking* was an old-fashioned word. It sounded almost quaint in this day and age, when women smoked on the street and men kept their hats on in elevators. But it was the perfect word for the couple in her binoculars. Young lovers frolicking in the surf. Catherine turned away, not wanting to intrude. Margaret, four years old, was tugging at her skirt, wanting to look, too. The older girls, Anne and Cathy, ten and eight, were at school in Westerly, and Geoffrey . . . She began fretting. Geoffrey was at it again. He was just reaching the defiant adolescent stage, and he was determined to be independent.

An hour later the Coast Guard called. Both boats were missing. Retrieving the binoculars over Margaret's protests, Catherine scanned the bay again. She picked out a speck on the horizon that could be Geoffrey and Andy. The Moores' cabin cruiser was anchored at the Watch Hill Yacht Club. The *Mageanca*, a name made up of the first two letters of their children's names: MArgaret, GEoffrey, ANne, and CAthy, was forty-two feet, and Catherine was petite, barely over five feet. It was too big for her to handle alone. She called her husband at the mill.

Westerly is roughly six miles west of Watch Hill. In ten minutes Jeff Moore was at the yacht club, taking the *Mageanca* out into Little Narragansett Bay. He headed for the point, motoring at full throttle, churning a high wake. The water was white-capped, as foamy as ale poured out too fast.

The *Mageanca* caught up with Geoffrey, Andy, and the runaway sailboat out at the clam flats at the end of the sandspit, where the water was shallow for some distance. Jeff turned the boat and backed into the flats, trying to maneuver close enough for the boys to wade out. The big cruiser ran aground, and they had to flag down another boat to tow them off. By the time they finally got home, the wind was whipping and the waves in the bay were two and three feet, higher than they had ever seen them.

At lunch Geoffrey began describing the wild chase to his mother. It was a sleigh ride out to the point, and Geoffrey enjoyed every minute of it. He never stopped to wonder how he would get back until he had snagged Anne's sailboat and tried to turn around. He was rowing hard just to hold his position. Realizing that they could never make it back, he and Andy dragged the boats up on the sand. As they started walking home, Andy spotted the *Mageanca*.

Geoffrey was in the middle of the story when his father suddenly turned an ashy white, clutched his chest, and slumped over the lunch table. Jeff Moore was much bigger than his wife or his son, and a good forty pounds heavier than Andy. Somehow, though, they managed to get him from the dining room, across the hall, into the living room, and onto the couch. Catherine gave him a shot of brandy to revive him and tried to take his pulse. It was so faint, she telephoned the doctor. As she dialed, she was thinking, *Could anything else go wrong today?*

———

That same morning on the island of Jamestown, after the school bus had picked up his children, Joe Matoes ferried his truck across the bay to deliver his milk in Newport. Matoes made his rounds every other day, stopping at the downtown restaurants, then swinging by the mansions along Bellevue Avenue and around Ocean Drive, dropping off bottles at the few houses that were still open. He finished his milk route around two o'clock. Although the sun was bright, the wind was whipping and surf was breaking over the seawall on Ocean Drive.

Matoes caught the 2:30 P.M. ferry home. It was a rough ride, much rougher than the morning run. The boat was more crowded than usual. Workers from Newport, concerned that a northeaster was coming, were trying to beat the storm home and the first rush of teenagers was returning from Rogers High in Newport. Jamestown didn't have a high school of its own. Matoes watched them from a distance — his niece Marge Matoes, Bill Chellis from the lighthouse, and maybe a dozen more — noisy, boisterous, so different from his own children. The *Governor Carr* pitched and yawed in the heavy sea, but the teenagers were too busy raising their own ruckus to notice the one on the bay. The girls were laughing, trying to hold down their skirts without dropping their books, and the boys were cheering with each gust that thwarted their efforts.

If Matoes was thinking that his daughter Mary should have been one of those girls with an armful of books, dark ponytail flying in the stiffening wind, he kept it to himself. Joe ran the farm. His wife, Lily, ran the house, and she didn't think a girl needed more schooling. He couldn't argue that, and he needed an extra pair of hands on the farm. The work never ended, and there was so much of it, not just the heavy pasture work but the day-to-day chores: shoveling the coal, pumping the well water, chopping ice from the huge block with a pick.

Mary had loved school, though. She was at the top of her class every year. Maybe it would be different with Theresa and Dorothy, because Dotty was Lily's girl. They were both good students like Mary, always on the honor roll. Not much chance Joseph would go to Rogers, or want to. Matoes couldn't work the farm without his son — a good boy, gentle with his sisters, a hard worker, so tall now that Joe had to look up at him. Rose would be proud, he thought, if she could see their boy today.

Matoes was a simple man. His nature was practical, not poetic, and it was pure happenstance that he had married two women who were named for flowers. That was about all Rose and Lily had in common. Matoes turned into the wind. So many years had passed since Rose had died. Months would go by without a thought of her, then all at once, when he wasn't watching, she would come back so clearly, she could be standing beside him. Now there was Lily. She wasn't an easy woman, but she had never had an easy time, widowed when Dotty was a baby, then taking on somebody else's children, three of them. Eunice had been good for them, good for all of them, made them more of a family. Still, there was a divide — Lily's girls, Dotty and Eunice, and Rose's kids, Mary and Joseph and Theresa. At least the three of them had one another.

CHAPTER 7

A Bright Young Man

The twenty-first of September was a gorgeous day in D.C., so gorgeous that it was hard to imagine foul weather could be lurking anywhere nearby. At the Washington Weather Bureau, bright young men, perched on tall stools at high wooden desks with slanted tops like architect's tables, charted the day's outlook. Two rows of identical desks faced each other, and at a glance, the men sitting behind them appeared identical, too. They were dressed in dark three-piece suits, white shirts with starched collars and cuffs, and sober ties knotted firmly. None of them rolled up their sleeves or loosened their ties, or even took off their jackets while they worked.

Charles Pierce was one of those bright young men. On this Wednesday morning he was plucked from their ranks to present the day's weather maps at the noon forecast meeting. Pierce was filling in for a vacationing senior forecaster, and he was eager to make a good impression. He studied the morning charts closely. Conditions over the Northeast appeared strangely incoherent.

Thunderstorms over New York. Long Island was a steam bath. There was danger of serious flooding in central Connecticut and western Massachusetts. But Rhode Island and eastern Connecticut were as sunny as Washington. A low-pressure system that stretched from New England to the Carolinas bore watching, and to the south the remains of the hurricane that had been threatening Florida for four days was prowling North Carolina's Outer Banks. Jacksonville had sent a couple of overnight advisories, all pertaining to the aborted hurricane. As advisories went, they were fairly mild, indicating no cause for alarm. Still, Pierce read them closely:

10:30 P.M.: Northeast storm warnings ordered from the Virginia Capes to Atlantic City, N.J., including lower Chesapeake Bay. Northeast winds becoming strong and reaching gale force (39–54 m.p.h.) in the Virginia Capes section Wednesday and southern New Jersey coast late Wednesday afternoon or Wednesday night.

4:00 A.M. update: Indications are center of hurricane will pass near but slightly off Carolina Capes within next 12 hours attended by dangerous gales and high tides on coast and by hurricane winds (75 m.p.h. plus) a short distance off shore. Storm warnings displayed north of Wilmington, N.C., to Atlantic City, N.J. Caution advised ships in path of this severe storm.

When the D.C. forecasters began tracking the storm about five A.M., it appeared to be slowing again. Like Norton and Dunn in Jacksonville, they believed it would follow the path of most North Atlantic hurricanes and curve out to sea. At 7:30 A.M., the system was some 140 miles east-northeast of Cape Hatteras, latitude 35° north, longtitude 73° west. The D.C. night crew downgraded the storm to a tropical disturbance. In their early-morning forecast, they noted only: *"A broad trough of low pressure extends from New England south-southwestward to the tropical disturbance. Pressure remains high from Nova Scotia and Newfoundland and southward and southeastward over the ocean."* They did not indicate a hurricane on the morning weather map that went out to regional newspapers and radio stations.

Following their lead, Charles Pierce issued an equally sanguine advisory about ten o'clock:

> *Hoist northeast storm warnings 10 A.M. DST north of Atlantic City and south of Block Island, R.I., and hoist southeast storm warnings Block Island to Eastport, Me. Tropical storm approximately central about 75 miles east of Cape Hatteras moving rapidly north-northeast attended by shifting gales over wide area and by winds of hurricane force near center. Northeast or north gales backing to northwest south of Block Island to Hatteras today and southeast or east gales Block Island to Eastport becoming northwest tonight or Thursday morning. Small craft should remain in port until storm passes.*

Through the morning, though, as he computed the statistical data and analyzed the surface charts, Pierce began to question the earlier assumptions. By his reckoning, the storm was east of Norfolk, Virginia, moving rapidly north again and still very much a hurricane. In the upper atmosphere above Washington, southerly winds of forty to fifty miles an hour were blowing. Since the storm was only about three hundred miles southeast, it was probably being pushed by similar winds. If his calculations were correct, the storm would blow on a straight track north from Hatteras. If it stayed on course without dissipating, the first landfall would be Long Island, six hundred miles away.

Looking back, Pierce would call the Great New England Hurricane "one of the most unusual, and from the viewpoint of the meteorologist, one of the most interesting storms in history. Because of the peculiar temperature and wind distribution in the upper atmosphere, instead of following its normal course, it moved straight northward over what, at that time, was the most densely populated area in the world." But that was in hindsight. On September 21 he was a junior forecaster, green and unsure, working for an agency that in many ways was stalled in the nineteenth century.

When the United States established its first official Weather Bureau, the director, Willis L. Moore, complained to Congress that his forecasters were under such intense pressure that they had "the highest rate of insanity of any government agency." The *Denver Republican* was one source of irritation. The newspaper routinely ran the official Weather Bureau forecast side by side with the predictions of ninety-year-old Oliver P. Wiggins. Wiggins would consult his bum left leg, wounded when he was scouting for Kit Carson, then issue his forecast. Wiggins's bum leg beat the Bureau so consistently, the newspaper was asked to stop the practice.

In 1938 the Weather Bureau still resembled a seat-of-the-pants enterprise more than a scientific laboratory. In many ways it lagged behind its European counterparts. In wartime, weather is often a determining factor in victory or defeat. The lessons of history are numerous: the Spanish Armada was caught in a gale; the sun came out at Austerlitz for Napoleon; a snowstorm delayed air cover in the Battle of the Bulge. Not surprisingly, then, war is a major catalyst that pushes science to make sense of the weather. Spurred by World War I, European meteorologists, particularly in Norway, pioneered a new type of synoptic forecasting based on air mass analysis and the influence of weather fronts. The United States was slow to adopt the new science.

A confidential report on the state of the U.S. Weather Bureau completed in January 1938 cited an "urgent need for modernization." Warning that the agency lacked a solid scientific basis, the report stated:

> The Forecast Division, while reasonably efficient administratively, does not have a technical staff, not even one person formally trained as a scientist. At the present time, there is a complete lack of any plan or method for systematic training of would-be official forecasters. It is a sorry state of affairs when candidates for such a responsible position are obliged to shift for themselves, picking up scraps of information as best they can. Unless a drastic change of policy is affected, it is certain that the Weather Bureau can progress only to a very limited extent and consequently will be deficient in the performance of its duty to render the best possible service to the public.

By September, few if any of the recommended changes had been implemented. Promising young candidates such as Pierce received no formal instruction. Sitting in on a forecast meeting was as close to on-the-job training as they got. Junior forecasters submitted "practice" forecasts, which were then compared with the official outlook. For ambitious young analysts, the meetings were a time to score points. But if their maps were off a degree or

less, if they differed from the official weather map, or if their con-
clusions were weakly grounded, they could feel disconcertingly
like Christians in the Colosseum.

When the noon meeting convened, Pierce's forecast was clearly
at odds with the prevailing outlook. To justify his radically different
analysis, he had drawn his charts precisely, and he pointed out a
couple of peculiar features. First, he cited the *Carinthia*'s dangerous
low-pressure reading. It indicated that the storm was still a full-
blown hurricane. Second, he noted, the Bermuda High was in an
unusual position. It had sidled north to latitude 44°. Normally
in September, it was around latitude 30–35°. According to his
calculations, the misplaced High would draw the storm north.
Analyses of upper-air patterns supported his contention. To the
west, a second front hung over the Alleghenies. Between the
parallel systems, a valley of low pressure extended from New
England to the Carolinas. This moist low-pressure channel had
turned the Northeast into a steam bath. After four days of unre-
lenting rain and oppressive humidity, New England was as close
to the tropics as it ever got. The trough was an open invitation to
a tropical cyclone.

Pierce thought his charts pointed to a disaster in the making.
A storm of hurricane force was hightailing it out of North Carolina and speeding up the Atlantic coast. If it was blocked from
going to sea by the unusual location of the Bermuda High and
blocked from blowing west by the parallel front over the Alleghenies, it would be sucked into the inviting channel between them.
Like a toboggan in a chute, it would have an unrestricted speed
zone leading directly into the heart of New England.

If Pierce assumed that anyone reading his charts would reach
a similar conclusion, he was sadly mistaken. In the opinion of the
D.C. veterans, the brash young man was whistling Dixie. Charles

Mitchell, chief of forecasting at the Bureau, was beyond a doubt the best forecaster in the Washington station — some would argue the best in the entire Weather Bureau. Short in stature, he had a long, oval face; a broad, domed forehead; and receding gray hair that he plastered down and combed to the side. His tongue was as sharp as the part in his hair.

Mitchell considered the young upstart through his wire-rimmed pince-nez. He had been predicting the weather since Pierce was in knickers. Backed by his senior forecast team, he dismissed the storm as a typical Cape Verde blow. The pattern was predictable. The cyclone would continue its curve and curl out to sea, where it would dwindle to a gale in the cold northern waters. A hurricane happened in balmy Gulf waters or the sultry Caribbean, not north of the Forty-third Parallel in icebound New England. Water temperatures there rarely reach 79°, the minimum needed to sustain a tropical cyclone.

Mitchell and his men had tracked dozens of Atlantic hurricanes, and none of them had ever made landfall north of Cape May. Furthermore, the system was weakening. Overnight it had gone from a Category 5 to a Category 3. They were counting on the high-pressure bank over the Alleghenies to hold the storm offshore while it continued making its predictable turn to the sea. It would peter out completely as it moved into the polar latitudes. The hurricane was a "one-hundred-year storm," they assured Pierce — all show and no action. In other words, the odds that it would strike land were a hundred to one.

Experience and precedent were on Mitchell's side. The evidence supported Pierce. The *Carinthia*'s low-pressure reading and the unusual northern position of the Bermuda High were clear alarms, but the veteran forecasters could not believe what was in front of their eyes. Experience trumped facts. As of September 21,

1938, New England had experienced only two major hurricanes in its three-hundred-year history. If it hadn't happened in more than a century, what were the odds it would happen today?

The Great September Gale of 1815

The last hurricane to reach New England was the Great September Gale of 1815. Described as the worst natural disaster "since the settlement of the country," the gale flattened New York and New England. Meadows close to the shoreline were covered in so much sand, they looked like beaches, and newspapers did not have enough columns to list all the ships that were lost.

In Reading, Massachusetts, just outside Boston, the Reverend Ralph Waldo Emerson lost the steeple of his church. In Amherst, lexicographer Noah Webster lost most of his apple orchards, and in Concord six-year-old Oliver Wendell Holmes lost his favorite pantaloons. He remembered the loss years later in a poem:

Lord! how the ponds and rivers boiled!
They seemed like bursting craters!
And oaks lay scattered on the ground
As if they were p'taters
And all above was in a howl,
And all below a clatter,
The earth was like a frying-pan,
Or some such hissing matter.

It chanced to be our washing-day,
And all our things were drying;
The storm came roaring through the lines,
And set them all a flying;

I saw the shirts and petticoats
Go riding off like witches;
I lost, ah! bitterly I wept, —
I lost my Sunday breeches!

I saw them straddling through the air,
Alas! too late to win them;
I saw them chase the clouds, as if
The devil had been in them;
They were my darlings and my pride,
My boyhood's only riches, —
"Farewell, farewell," I faintly cried, —
"My breeches! O my breeches!"

That night I saw them in my dreams,
How changed from what I knew them!
The dews had steeped their faded threads,
The winds had whistled through them!
I saw the wide and ghastly rents
Where demon claws had torn them;
A hole was in their amplest part,
As if an imp had worn them.

I have had many happy years,
And tailors kind and clever,
But those young pantaloons have gone
Forever and forever!
And not till fate has cut the last
Of all my earthly stitches,
This aching heart shall cease to mourn
My loved, my long-lost breeches!

In Stonington, Connecticut, the tide rose seventeen feet higher than the highest tide and swept across the town. Everything was washed from the wharves, and then the wharves themselves were demolished. Neighboring Napatree — or Nap-o-tree, as it was called in 1815 — was densely forested. The September Gale wiped it clean, and no tree has grown there since.

Reginald E. Peck related in *Early Landholders of Watch Hill:* "Dame Nature smote the coast with a terrible gale which did irreparable damage from which the shore line never recovered. It was this gale which denuded the Naps of its thick woods and reduced it in size to its present width."

Another local commentator, the Reverend Frederic A. Denison, described "the big wind" in *Westerly and Its Witnesses:* "The ocean wave, raised by the gale, rose ten feet along the coast from the shore meadows, and swelled the river [Pawcatuck] nine feet above its usual height at the head of tidewater. Two porpoises were driven up into the village. The spray from the sea was driven far back into the country [and] all the forests on the coast were prostrated."

Narragansett Bay surged over its banks, washing away the stores on Newport's Long Wharf Street and killing a family of five. In Providence, 11.9 feet of water turned the downtown area into a lake, and four ships, nine brigs, seven schooners, and fifteen sloops were carried away. Moses Brown, a leading Rhode Island merchant, was said to have lost $1 million, a kingly sum. Virtually the entire downtown had to be rebuilt, which turned out to be a boon. Substantial brick buildings replaced the ramshackle warehouses. At the foot of College Hill, Providence, on a corner of the Old Market House, a plaque marks the high-water point. The record of 11.9 feet stood for 122 years and 363 days — until September 21, 1938.

After the storm, Long Island neighbors Daniel Hopping and William Miller were comparing their losses. "Well, Mr. Miller," said Hopper, "the Lord was in my field of corn the other night." "That may be true," Miller replied, "but the Devil was in mine."

On September 21, 1938, history would repeat itself. The simi larities between 1815 and 1938 are extraordinary. Both the Great September Gale and the Great Hurricane were born off the Cape Verde Islands, followed virtually identical paths from the Bahamas, and made landfall on Long Island within ten miles of each other. Both came at the end of unusually wet and humid summers. June 1938 was the third-wettest in New England weather records, and the September rains left the region waterlogged. The two storms struck when it was both high tide and the highest tide of the year — during the autumnal equinox, when the sun and moon are aligned with the earth, causing a double gravitational pull and producing the highest tides.

On September 23, 1815, and again on September 21, 1938, everything in nature — temperature, tides, air currents, and seasonal rainfall — conspired to make New England the perfect place for a hurricane.

CHAPTER 8

Upside Down, Inside Out

Usually September is New England's golden month — brilliant days, breezy nights, and the sweet dream of an Indian summer. Temperatures are mellow, warm but without the intense heat of July and August. Zinnias, dahlias, and goldenrod are in bloom, the last of the berries are bright on the bush, and overhead the first trace of autumn colors the trees. Fat puffs of cumulus drift across the sky, and off the coast striped bass and tuna swim in crowded schools. The occasional gale, or "line storm," that sends breakers crashing onto rocky coasts and vaulting seawalls adds a quotient of drama to the glorious days.

But the summer of '38 had been miserable. Weeks had been either soggy or scorching. Record rains in June and July, record heat in August. No one could remember a worse season. Twenty-seven August days had been hotter than normal, and long after dark, families sat out on porches and stoops, fanning themselves with folded newspapers, trying to catch a breeze. Women hiked their skirts up over their knees, and men stripped to their undershirts while children slept on screened-in porches, hair plastered against flushed cheeks.

In September the rains had returned, bringing muggy, gray days of on-again, off-again showers. Nothing dried, body and spirit felt permanently dampened, and mildew sprouted everywhere — on bread, in grouting, on the clothes in the hamper. Spirits sagged. Hair frizzed. Summer tans faded. Sewers clogged.

By mid-month, the weather was upside down, inside out — monsoons in Hartford, tropical heat in Newport — and the Atlantic felt like a bathtub. Across the Northeast, dismal days turned to deluges. The drenching had started on Saturday, the seventeenth of September: Drizzle in the morning. A noontime thunderclap. Thunderstorms again for dinner. A downpour through the night. Rain, rain, and more rain for four days straight. Sunday had dropped 3 inches on eastern Long Island and 2.5 inches on Hartford. The Connecticut River rose to precarious levels. Monday brought more of the same. In New York City the workweek began in a dense fog. Skyscrapers dissolved in the ether, while the city below steamed under 100 percent humidity. Rumbling thunderstorms at noon and again at rush hour brought no relief. The total rainfall for the day, 1.8 inches, equaled the rain in Hartford, and another 1.5 inches fell overnight. More than 3 inches soaked both Atlantic City, New Jersey, and Bridgeport, Connecticut.

Tuesday had been even wetter: 3 inches in Bridgehampton, Long Island; 5.36 inches in New Haven; another 3.5 inches in Hartford; 5.6 inches in Hillsborough, New Hampshire. Around Hartford, the Connecticut River rose a foot every three or four hours. Quiet tributaries became white-water rapids. Dams burst. In Willimantic the river flooded, severely damaging the American Thread Company, the town's major employer. Overnight another 3.2 inches fell in Hartford, bringing the total to more than 6 inches in twenty-four hours. Connecticut and Massachusetts braced themselves for even more rain. Corner grocers commiserated with customers. Neighbors fretted over back fences. Conversations were as predictable as the day's forecast. *Wet enough for you? Never saw a September like this one. What is the world coming to? Just imagine if this were snow.*

After such a sustained drenching, the most unusual thing about Wednesday, the twenty-first, was the appearance of the sun in southern New England. It seemed like a perfect morning for a picnic on the rocks, a game of golf, or hanging the laundry out to dry. In hindsight, though, the morning would seem too perfect, the perfection itself a presage. The absence of gulls, the cirrus clouds, the preternatural stillness, the exceptionally long ocean swells, were all portents that no one read in time. The colors of the day were a tip-off, too, and the voice of the wind.

When the shift in the weather came, it was swift and dramatic. About noon the day began to feel heavy, as if it had changed from lawn cotton into wool, and the wind stole in. At first, it was a nuisance — slamming doors, knocking a jar of zinnias off a window ledge. If you put anything down, it disappeared. By midafternoon the Atlantic turned a sulky gray. The sky took on a jaundiced cast, and wind gusted out of the southeast in strong bursts that sent the cirrus threads scudding. It ripped out wisteria vines and toppled fences. All along the Northeast coast, riled by the wind, the sea became magnificent and mad.

In inland towns and cities, where the weather did not dictate the day's activities, radios were tuned into CBS Studio Nine. Correspondent William Shirer was reporting from Berlin that Hitler had just won his first slice of Czechoslovakia. At eleven o'clock, under intense pressure from Britain and France to concede or fight alone, the Czechs had capitulated. Was it "peace in our time," or a "base betrayal"? CBS correspondent Ed Murrow was standing by in London for a live broadcast with Anthony Eden.

No weather advisories interrupted the program.

CHAPTER 9

Battening the Hatches

At two o'clock, the *Bostonian* reached New Haven. A misty rain was falling. The awning on the newspaper stand was snapping, and a porter's red cap was skipping down the platform. Disembarking passengers disappeared in billows of steam. Because New Haven was a main switching station, there was always an extended delay there. Two or three cars were decoupled to go on to Hartford while the main train continued to Boston. The switch took about twenty minutes. By the time the *Bostonian* pulled out of the station, at approximately 2:20 P.M., engineer Harry Easton was sure something big was brewing.

In the best of weather, the ocean is just yards from the railbed that runs through southern Connecticut between New Haven and Westerly, Rhode Island. After so many days and nights of rain, washouts were a danger, and now gusting winds and rain increased the hazard, forcing Easton to reduce speed. The *Bostonian* reached New London half an hour late. As the train idled in the station, waiting for a lull in the wind, a gray veil seemed to drop over the harbor. Beneath the whitecapped surface, the water appeared pewter-colored and oddly menacing. Passengers sitting on the seaward side of the train could see small skiffs and dories capsizing. Yachts were rocking furiously, like cradles pushed by crazed nannies, and trawlers strained at their moorings. The water was breaking over the road and inching closer to the tracks.

All along the scenic Northeast coast, the weather worsened by the moment. Gale force winds and driving rain in New York. Flooding throughout Connecticut. Although it was still sunny and 75° in Rhode Island, winds were gusting in Providence and the seas in Narragansett Bay were big and choppy. To New Englanders who had lived all their lives on the coast, the Atlantic was their front yard. They knew its moods and the weather it brought. As the afternoon turned threatening, most of them assumed it was weather as usual. They mistook the approaching gale for the familiar line storms that come every September, the signal that, thousands of miles away, the sun is dipping below the equator. The fall equinox marked the change from summer to autumn as clearly as the removal of summer slipcovers or the first day of school.

Old salts eyed the chameleon day and tightened mooring lines. Neighbors gathered on the beaches to enjoy the spectacle — to marvel at the odd mustardy sky and the magnificent rolling breakers. When the wind started banging on their beach house windows and the first rain oozed under sills and doorjambs, they "snugged up" and battened the hatches with the high spirits they usually displayed when preparing a clambake. They rolled up the rugs and got out the mops. They shut all the windows, stuffed them with Turkish towels, and shored up the doors with whatever heavy object was handy.

———

In the school yard in Jamestown, Joseph Matoes looked through the window of the school bus at the wind rippling the water in the puddles. The puddle water was moving so fast that it looked as if some unseen hand were stirring it. In the open pastures of Fox Hill Farm, the wind would be undoing all the work of the early morning. Joseph looked out at the clusters of concerned parents waiting to pick up their children, wondering if he would get home in time to help his father finish the haying before the storm started.

The school yard was unusually crowded. Children who always walked home found their mothers or fathers waiting outside for them. Fred Clarke, who was in the sixth grade with Joseph Matoes and Clayton Chellis, remembers that his father picked him up and drove him down to the bay to pull his rowboat out of the water. "It looked like a good northeaster was coming, nothing we hadn't seen before, though. I dragged the boat across the street from the yacht club and tied it to a gate, thinking it would be perfectly safe there. Around five o'clock, when things really started to pop, we drove back to check on the boat. All that was left was the rope." Patty Miller's mother picked her up early from kindergarten and they drove to Beavertail to collect their friend Ernest Chapman, a landscape painter who had gone out to the lighthouse to paint the wild sea. The Millers' car would be the last one to make it back safely from Beavertail. Billy Ordiner's mother picked him up at school, too, and they drove out to the lighthouse to see the surf. Billy was in the seventh grade. He and his mother would start back after the Millers and get as far as Mackerel Cove.

Like so many Jamestown parents, Joe Matoes was worried by the ominous weather. When the 2:30 P.M. ferry from Newport docked, he drove the three or four short blocks to the school. Matoes just missed his children. Joseph, Theresa, Dotty, and Eunice had left on the school bus a few minutes earlier.

Out on Fort Road, Napatree, Dr. Fernald Fitts was completing a house call. He was standing on the Moores' porch, holding on to his hat. Bracing himself against the wind, he told Catherine Moore that her husband, Jeff, had suffered a mild heart attack and needed three days of complete bed rest. "No excitement," he said. "No exertion."

When Dr. Fitts left, Catherine went upstairs to Jeff, still trying to absorb the shock. What a day! First the runaway sailboat and the mad chase to the end of the bay, then the *Mageanca* beached and towed, and now Jeff. A heart attack at thirty-eight. Jeff was an extrovert, a consummate salesman, and always a keen competitor. He'd been an athlete when they met. A star fullback and captain of the football team at Westerly High, he had gone on to play semi-pro football with the Providence Steamrollers, under coach Jimmy Crowley, one of the famous Four Horsemen of Notre Dame. Jeff's three great loves were his family, football, and boats.

Glancing out their bedroom window, Catherine saw their Herreshoff break away from its mooring. Dragging anchor, the sailboat moved slowly but steadily down the bay. A light rain was falling. Before the boat reached the fort, the rain was a solid sheet across the water. Catherine went to check the other upstairs windows. Water was blowing in under the sills and dripping down from the window tops. She ran for towels and bath mats. As she worked frantically to keep up with the water, Jeff called from his sickbed, "There goes Cy's boat."

When the two older Moore girls got home from school a few minutes later, there was a chair from the beach club in their front yard, the downstairs rugs were rolled up, and Geoffrey's steamer trunk with his new school clothes was sitting on top of his bed. Anne and Cathy raced into the house, talking a mile a minute about their ride home from school. They almost didn't make it. They had to dodge fallen trees and telegraph poles, and the wind gusts were so strong that the car almost blew off the road.

CHAPTER 10

A One-Hundred-Year Storm

Back at his desk in the Washington Weather Bureau with the rest of the bright young forecasters, a chastened Charlie Pierce was keeping an anxious watch over the speeding storm. He was the only one. In the 2:00 P.M. advisory from Washington, forecasting chief Charles Mitchell, not a man to be second-guessed, deleted the word *hurricane* from the weather update. The edited forecast read only: *Northerly winds along the New Jersey, Maryland and southern Delaware coast will likely increase to whole gale force this afternoon and back to northwest and diminish tonight.* The advisory was sent out to weather posts, newspaper offices, and radio stations in the Northeast at two o'clock. Half an hour later, at approximately 2:30 P.M., against odds of a hundred to one and confounding all conventional wisdom, the Great Hurricane of 1938 came ashore.

A one-hundred-year storm is one of the most misunderstood terms in meterology. It refers to a hurricane that in a given year has a 1 percent probability of striking a particular stretch of land. Although this may sound unlikely, the Great Hurricane of 1938 was such a storm. It was the most destructive natural disaster in U.S. history — worse than the San Francisco earthquake, the Chicago fire, or any Mississippi flood.

As swift and sure as a Joe Louis punch, the hurricane darted up the Atlantic coast at fifty, sixty, and seventy miles an hour, faster than most cars could travel in 1938. No hurricane had ever raced as fast. It arrived unannounced. It struck without warning, and it showed no mercy. Entire beach communities that seemed secure at lunchtime were wiped off the map by supper. At 3:30 P.M. on Napatree, the Moores were battening the hatches and marveling at the spectacle of the rolling breakers. Fifteen minutes later, at 3:45 P.M., vertical walls of water, two and three stories high, were plowing through the cement seawall as if it were transparent. "All I could see outside the second-floor bedroom windows was the spume and froth on the underneath part of the waves," Geoffrey Moore's aunt Harriet remembered. "The waves were breaking over the top of the house and we were under them."

Viewed from the serenity of space, a hurricane looks like a swirl of marshmallow frosting on a cupcake. Observed from within, it is "dazzling sunlight and bright blue sky." Meteorologist Robert Simpson, one of the first to fly through the eye of a hurricane, described it vividly:

The plane flew through bursts of torrential rain and several turbulent bumps. Then, suddenly, we were in dazzling sunlight and bright blue sky. Around us was an awesome display. The eye was a clear space 40 miles in diameter surrounded by a coliseum of clouds whose walls on one side rose vertically and on the other were banked like the galleries in a great opera house. The upper rim, about 35,000 feet high, was rounded off smoothly against a background of blue sky. Below us was a floor of low clouds rising to a dome 8,000 feet above sea level in the center. There were breaks in it that gave us glimpses of the surface of the ocean. In the vortex of the eye, the sea was a scene of unimaginably violent, churning water.

Experienced from below, an extreme hurricane is a sudden explosion of wind and water. It is Nature flaunting its supremacy and cutting us down to size, reducing our finest creations to rubble, knocking us back centuries.

Town by town, the Northeast darkened and was silenced. The brilliant inventions of modern life were knocked out. Phones failed. Lights failed. Cars flooded. Buses and trolleys stalled. Trains derailed. Long Island could not alert Connecticut. Connecticut could not warn Rhode Island. Each community stood alone, isolated against the onslaught. What had been assumed permanent was lost, and the familiar was made strange.

Houses went to sea, boats came ashore, and ordinary objects were recast. A safe harbor became a cemetery; the family car, a tomb. Rooftops were rafts. A shingle became a deadly projectile. A pier, wrenched from its pilings, became a battering ram. A rough-hewn twelve-foot-square cabin glowed like a palace. Salvation and destruction, redemption and death were as random as the flip of a coin, and the air was so thick with salt and murky spray that day was as blind as night.

Ponds turned into white-ruffled seas. Waves appeared sky-high. Geography, topography, the lay of the land, became critical factors. The surging water washed out bridges, eroded railbeds, and buckled highways. It rolled cars like drunks in a dark alley, sank them in tidal ponds, carried them out to sea, and flooded them in city streets. The ancient elms that canopied Main Streets, the white church steeples that had defined the landscape of New England since colonial days, all fell. Memories, landmarks, family treasures, washed away — and still the tide rose.

Trains and tankers were tossed aside like Tinkertoys. Waves as high as fifty feet swept homes and families into the sea. Mothers strapped their babies onto mattresses, launched them on the rampaging sea, and prayed. Sea spray was flung like fusillade, and windowpanes in Montpelier, Vermont, 120 miles from the sea, were coated with salt.

Wealthy families in oceanfront mansions and fishermen's families in tar-paper shacks, prep school boys and college coeds returning to school for the new year were caught in the storm. Even when they were trapped in the surge of wind and water, many never realized what was happening to them — and those who did could not believe it. No one in the Northeast had ever witnessed such a tumult or heard such an uproar. The noise was deafening — a cacophony of short-circuited trolley bells and car horns, the shriek of the wind, the din of a world being sundered. Decades later the most vivid memories remained those of color and sound.

Howard Smith, a ten-year-old paperboy in 1938, remembered "a unique and strangely tinted day." His father, an artist, was intrigued by the layers of color on the afternoon:

The sky changed to a rich greenish yellow. The green appeared murky, and the yellow transparent. All seemed glazed over with a very light and delicate golden red. Though it was still calm, we could hear a weird hollow noise coming from some indefinable distant place. Deep and steady and musical, but also eerie and impossible to locate, the sound was frightening. Haunting and disorienting, it seemed to be everywhere and nowhere in particular. For all I knew, the sound could have been coming from the earth or myself or the sky. As time went on, the sound grew louder, more hollow, carrying greater reverberations.

Floreann Martin, twenty-four, was vacationing in Hyannis with her husband:

In the morning it was beautiful. The sun was out with very high winds because I remember I had a wide skirt on and I had a time with it. Then it got very, very calm suddenly, as though somebody had turned the switch off and then it got overcast. The rains came, and the winds kept picking up and picking up. Of course, we had no idea it was a hurricane. No warnings — nothing. And the wires — I must tell you about the wires. Edgar Allan Poe could have described it so well. They were screaming like a woman in the night — a high, high pitch. The wind was catching the wires and it was the eeriest sound. If Poe weren't my favorite author, I think I would have had chills up to here listening to the scream of those wires. We had the accelerator right to the floor, and we were doing fifteen miles an hour because the wind was pushing us back.

Wind is simply air in motion. The notion conjures refreshing images — a sail billowing on a summer day, the rustle of autumn leaves, the free, fresh wind in your hair — until you bump up against air that's moving at hurricane speed. A wind of 155 miles an hour feels as if you have collided with fifty bull elephants. It packs the force of three hundred tons. No one will ever know the strength of the winds in the Great Hurricane of 1938, because they destroyed every instrument designed to measure them. Before it blew, the anemometer at the Blue Hill Observatory in Milton, Massachusetts, some seventy miles from the eye of the storm, recorded gusts of 186 miles per hour and a sustained wind of 121 miles per hour. It was the second-highest rate ever recorded in the Northern Hemisphere.

On Long Island, the wind sandblasted every bit of paint off one side of Bill Crapser's brand-new 1938 Chevrolet coupe and left the other side pristine. In Ledyard, Connecticut, it picked up fourteen-year-old Vivian Avery Williams when she came out of the one-room schoolhouse and sent her somersaulting down the road. Strong men, if they could walk at all, were bent perpendicular, their noses almost touching the sidewalk. Oliver Stedman, an electrical contractor, crawled up Sugar Loaf Hill in Wakefield, Rhode Island, on his hands and knees. It was the only way he could get home. "I had to crawl," he said, "the wind was blowing so hard. I would have been blown right over into the woods."

At the peak of the hurricane, the world became wind and the wind, the world. It surrounded you, owned you. It hummed, whistled, whined, keened, screeched. Everyone who heard it was struck deaf and mute. Its voice was incessant, exhausting, encompassing. It was impossible to think above its clamor, to hear or be heard. Immovable objects met its irresistible force and surrendered. It caused rain to slash and sea spray to bite; it took your breath away, then choked you with rain and spindrift. Breathing in was like swallowing shrapnel.

The Great Hurricane of 1938 made landfall at Patchogue, Long Island, striking with such force that it set off seismographs in Alaska.

CHAPTER 11

How Do You Lose a Hurricane?

As the crow flies, the distance from Cape Hatteras to Long Island is 425 miles, and the Hurricane of 1938 covered it in seven hours. Speeding up the coast with such velocity that New Yorkers nicknamed it the "Long Island Express," the hurricane sideswiped New Jersey. By two o'clock, sea spray was flying over the Steel Pier in Atlantic City. Huge combers washed over the beaches of Wildwood, Manasquan, and Point Pleasant and tore up miles of famous boardwalks along the Jersey Shore. On the truck farms of South Jersey, gale-force winds beat the last beefsteak tomatoes of the season to pulp; sucked the sweet corn dry, leaving fields of brown husks as brittle as old paper; and picked the apple orchards clean. The smell of applesauce hung in the air for weeks, attracting droves of yellow jackets.

The western edge of the storm skirted New York City — a degree or two of difference in longitude and Manhattan would have been devastated. The glancing blow pelted the city with rain and wind. Heavy morning thunderstorms turned to monsoons by afternoon. Gusts as high as 120 miles an hour screamed from the top of the Empire State Building and thirty-miles-per-hour winds swirled down the avenues. Street signs swung. Billboards toppled. Garbage cans tipped and rolled, clanging down the streets. The afternoon commute became a nightmare. Subways flooded. Trolleys stalled. The Empire State Building swayed four inches.

At the southern tip of Manhattan, the flag on the U.S. Weather Bureau office shredded like ticker tape, and the station's barometer nose-dived. By 3:50 P.M. it read 28.72, a record low for September. Harbor waters were sloshing over the Battery by the time the Staten Island ferry *Knickerbocker* cut her engine and began backing slowly into her slip. Severe winds and a quick succession of waves broadsided the heavy vessel and slammed her up against the pilings. The overhanging deck snagged on the top of the piles, and the ferry tipped like a seesaw. There were 220 passengers aboard and more waiting on the Battery dock, most of them screaming in terror. Tilting at a precarious 30° angle, the big boat shifted and thrashed in the rough waters. Her distress horn blared across the harbor. Two Standard Oil Company tugs answered the alarm, followed by a Coast Guard cutter, fireboats, and police launches. A garbled report that a ferry had capsized reached police headquarters, and scores of New York's finest swarmed downtown.

In midtown, the Cunard Line's opulent *Queen Mary*, scheduled to sail for Southampton at 4:30 P.M., never left her mooring. Most passengers and their guests stayed on board. Corks popped, champagne spurted like sea spray, and bon-voyage revelers partied through the night. On the Great White Way, the curtain was going up on the first new show of the season. Aptly titled *You Never Know*, the Cole Porter musical opened to a handful of dazed and sodden first-nighters. When the morning papers hit the newsstands, the composer probably wished the critics had not braved the elements. Over at Radio City Music Hall, it was the last night for *You Can't Take It with You.* The new Fred Astaire–Ginger Rogers musical *Carefree* was opening Thursday.

Blackouts pitched areas of Manhattan, Brooklyn, and the Bronx into darkness. In Queens, downed trees forced drivers to swerve onto sidewalks and across front lawns. Flooding was so severe that rowboats from the Central Park Boat Basin and dories from the Fulton Street Fish Market were rushed to the borough for emergency rescue duty. At the U.S. Tennis Open in Forest Hills, rain halted the semifinals match for the fifth time, frustrating the hopes of Don Budge for another day. Budge, a twenty-three-year-old redheaded giant from California, was trying to become the first player to win all four major tennis titles in the same year.

Another California champ was in town for the deluge. Just the day before, Seabiscuit, the never-say-die thoroughbred, had lost his first New York race of the year, the $6,050 Belmont Handicap, on the sloppy course. Conditions at Belmont Park were impossible now, but the horses were still running as scheduled. The track was a mud bath, and the course worsened with each race. By the final meet, the featured Westchester Claiming Stakes, the stands were empty. The rain was so thick, the timer could not see the flag drop at the starting gate. The horses ran untimed. The PA system was dead and the announcer was "shouting himself blue in the face" trying to call the race. Silks were dripping, the numbers unreadable, and all the horses — roans, grays, and chestnuts — were a uniform mud brown. Trainers and touts called it "the worst day ever anywhere," and the *New York Herald Tribune* reported that the jockeys "not only had mud and driving rain to contend with, but at times the wind seemed strong enough to blow the little fellows right off their saddles."

When the long shot At Play finally splashed across the finish line, knee-deep in slop, the Hurricane of 1938 was slamming into the Hamptons.

Should the Washington Weather Bureau have called the hurricane of 1938?

In 1627, Francis Bacon in his utopian fable *The New Atlantis* imagined a not-too-distant future when man would be master of the weather. Today, despite the best efforts to tame it through study and science, weather remains inscrutable. It seems that the more scientists learn about it, the more there is to discover, and the mystery deepens when it comes to predicting the behavior of a hurricane.

Even with today's supercomputers and mathematical models, it is impossible to re-create the conditions that caused a hurricane or to keep up with one in progress. Using data collected from satellites, scientists have tried to figure out how a hurricane develops. They have re-created the exact conditions of recent cyclones and then essentially pressed the rewind button, working backward from step C to B to A. Each time, as they retraced the steps from hurricane to tropical storm, to tropical depression, dangerous disturbance, and sinister cloud cluster, they eventually ended up with a set of atmospheric conditions indistinguishable from dozens of others.

Ernest Zebrowski Jr. defines the problem in his book *Perils of a Restless Planet:*

What is it that whips some of these minor atmospheric fluctuations into full-blown hurricanes, while others disperse after causing no more annoyance than blowing off someone's hat in Africa? It's impossible to say for sure. All we know is that this fundamental agent must be very small, because all of our expensive and sophisticated instrumentation can't detect it. We can see only so much detail, we can measure only to limited precision, and we can compute only to finite accuracy.

The answer to why hurricanes change speed and direction is equally elusive. "Experiments with computer simulations suggest that the future of a storm is always extremely sensitive to tiny fluctuations in what goes on within it," Zebrowski writes. Variations too minuscule to measure may seriously affect its course. Why one hurricane develops into a killer storm while another sputters out may depend on how the sun strikes the earth, the shift of the continents 10 million years ago, or that ill wind blowing across the Sahara. A day, a degree, even a thousandth of a degree, may make a dramatic difference.

Although it appears to be a random phenomenon — chaos loosed upon an unsuspecting land — even the fiercest cyclonic whirlwind is part of a weather machine so immense and intricate that some scientists believe we shall never achieve 100 percent accurate forecasts. We have split the atom, orbited the earth, touched down on the moon, and cracked the genetic code, yet after decades of study and with all the technological tools of the trade — radar, radiosonde, aerial reconnaissance, weather satellites, and mathematical computer models — we still cannot predict a hurricane more than twenty-four hours in advance.

In 1938 forecasters faced far greater odds. Jacksonville saw the storm coming. Tracked it closely. Issued three and four advisories each day. The southern states were on high alert. Relief groups and governmental agencies had emergency plans in place.

But forecasters had only six basic tools: three relatively recent inventions — the radio, telephone, and telegraph — and three seventeenth-century instruments — the thermometer, barometer, and hygrometer to measure humidity levels. They relied almost entirely on surface observations.

As long as the storm was in the Caribbean, the Bureau received frequent updates from weather posts on the islands. Once the hurricane reached the clear coastal waters of the Atlantic, though, the only reliable reports came from ships at sea. On the twenty-first, heeding the warnings from Jacksonville, most ships either stayed in port or went far out to sea; and unnoticed by all except Charlie Pierce, the hurricane found the low-pressure trough and was lured north.

The trough worked like a fishing line cast from New England to Cape Hatteras. An angry, murderous leviathan was hooked off Diamond Shoal. As the great beast was reeled in, its thrashing tail thumped the Jersey Shore and a fin slapped at New York. Diving over Fire Island, it beached on Long Island's South Shore, then it bounded over the island and crossed the Sound to New England.

CHAPTER 12

The Long Island Express

A ridge forms the spine of Long Island, west to east. The North Shore harbors the wealthy enclaves — Oyster Bay, Teddy Roosevelt's home, and the mythic Gatsby country. The South Shore, good for potato farming, is flat and sandy all the way from Fire Island and the Hamptons to Montauk at the tip.

As late as the 1920s, the region still belonged to fishermen and farmers, some old-money types needing to breathe free, and the last of the Old Dutch. But change was evident even then. P. T. Barnum had built the first hotel in the Hamptons in 1868, and the railroad came a few years later. The easy commute attracted the newer rich, who spilled out of Pullman cars in ever increasing numbers each summer.

By 1938, they had made the Hamptons their summer stomping grounds, snapping up the old farms and crowding vacation homes onto the sixty-mile stretch of barrier beach from Fire Island eastward to Southampton. Gerald and Sara Murphy, legendary expatriates (he the millionaire heir to Mark Cross leather goods, she the unnamed model for Picasso's white lady), were back in their East Hampton home after a European trip with John Dos Passes and his wife, Katy. Thanks to the miserable hothouse weather, their garden was a showcase. Gerald Murphy described it in a letter to Alexander Woollcott, the critic, actor, and wit:

> We had to Easthampton returned to find it glowing with tuberoses, bamboo, elephant ear, white heliotrope, nico-tiana — and Sara's brocades inside the house. She left it that Wednesday [September 21] having arranged her linen and lace chest and placed what we had dragged from abroad to perfect effect.

For the most part, though, the Hamptons were gray, deserted shore towns on Wednesday morning. At Westhampton Beach, the population had shrunk from a summer high of three thousand to about eight hundred — mostly the locals and the "colored help" left behind to close up the estates.

Tot and Norvin Greene summered at Westhampton Beach with their children, Gretchen and Gair. Their house was the last one on the bay side of Dune Road, about four miles west of the nearest bridge. Norvin, an investment banker, would take the train out after work on Wednesday and stay through Sunday. The Greenes planned to close their home that weekend. Gretchen and Gair were counting the days. This was the first summer that they were eager to get back to the city. Tot was ready to return, too. The season had been a disappointment — day after day of pouring rain or sweltering heat, and not much in between.

Gretchen and Gair woke up Wednesday morning feeling as sulky as the weather. Cooped up in the house again! There were no books to read and no games to play that they had not read and played a million times. They could recite whole pages of their favorite books by heart.

Thirty-year-old Tot Greene was as fed up with the miserable weather as her children. Pouring a second cup of coffee, she gazed out the breakfast room window, trying to think of something fun for them to do. Unlike the fine weather in southern New England, the twenty-first was another dismal morning on Long Island. Outside, the beach was empty. Not a soul, not even a bird. The sand was dark from the overnight rain, and the long blades of dune grass were bent almost parallel to it. The wind must be nasty. Not a day to go beachcombing, searching for sea glass, shells, and stones to bring back to the city.

Long, restless hours yawned ahead of them. Tot didn't want to hear another "What can we do now, Mom?" But she could not blame her children. When you're ten and eight, being housebound for weeks can make you antsy and irritable — even if your house is in the dunes of Westhampton Beach. Tot stepped to the phone and made some calls. She didn't want the summer to be a complete washout. Rain or no rain, the Greenes were going to have a party — an end-of-summer party. It would be a distraction for Gretchen and Gair and a chance to say good-bye to their summer friends until next year.

A couple of towns away in Bridgehampton, Ernest Clowes was watching the day closely. Clowes, a volunteer observer for the Weather Bureau, did not like what he saw. The morning had dawned misty and pale along the Long Island shore. Smothering air as thick as a poultice pressed down on the island. Overnight thunderstorms had brought no relief. The grand elms on Southampton's main street were dripping like showerheads. Even the easterly wind that was chopping at the waters of the Sound was blowing hot and sticky.

Offshore, the weather appeared benign enough. The Montauk fleet had gone out at dawn. But across the Sound at Stonington, Connecticut, a brick-red sunrise, the third in three days, kept the Portuguese fishermen in port mending their nets. To a fisherman, superstitions aren't so much ungrounded fears as a mixture of lore and experience — stories passed down with the requisite embroidering at every retelling, knowledge born of bad luck, or sage advice once brushed aside in the bravado of youth. Fishermen at the mercy of the mercurial sea learn caution and the perils of imprudence. In the lore of Portuguese fishermen, three consecutive red sunrises meant a wicked storm was on the way.

Clowes was not superstitious, but by noon he was apprehensive. The barometer was skidding down and the easterly wind had puffed up to a gale. At Moriches Inlet, between Fire Island and Westhampton, the Coast Guard was on patrol, warning the few hardy beachgoers to keep out of the water. Out at Westhampton Beach, parents dropping their children off at the Greenes' party stopped to admire the towering surf. They never thought that they were delivering their children into the clutch of a treacherous sea.

Because September often brought high winds and raucous seas, most Long Islanders assumed that wet and windy Wednesday was "a bad case of normalcy." Arthur Raynor, a year out of high school and still looking for work in 1938, put it this way: "Gray skies are no novelty in this part of the world, particularly at the fall equinox. 'Line storms' were an expected feature. The wind would haul around to the northeast, the rains would come in cold, nasty squalls, and once in a while a branch would break off somebody's tree. The leaves which were about to hit the ground were accelerated somewhat, and fall came in like a lion."

As skies glowered and winds howled, Ernest Clowes began to keep a detailed record of the day: "A little after one o'clock, it began to rain heavily," he noted. "By two o'clock gale winds were blowing and the barometer was sliding down." In two hours, the barometric pressure dropped from 29.78 to 27.43, and wind velocity soared. The warm noontime zephyr rose to forty miles an hour by 1:30 P.M.

Clowes telephoned the Weather Bureau station located on the Battery in Manhattan. Although he still had no thought of a hurricane, he wanted permission to spread the word that a serious September gale was approaching. While he was on the phone requesting authorization, the storm was rattling windows and generally causing havoc in Lower Manhattan. Even then, no one at the station had a clue that the rumpus outside was a hurricane. The two o'clock advisory from Washington — with the word *hurricane* deleted — reached the Manhattan weather station in tandem with the storm.

According to Ernest Clowes's time line, he phoned the Manhattan station at two o'clock. By 2:30, the storm was engulfing Fire Island, cutting a wide channel through the town of Saltaire and marooning residents. By three o'clock, the first trees were falling on Long Island, and at approximately 3:30, the hurricane arrived "in all its power and fury."

"The sky was darkened," Clowes wrote, "and the warm air was thick with a smother of rain, spray and all sorts of small items going by, almost horizontally, principally shreds of leaves torn in pieces from the trees. A barn, a chicken house, would lift from its foundations and collapse or burst into fragments that flew away down the wind." Toward four o'clock "the final catastrophe occurred. The sea surged. The whole barrier of the dunes crumbled. In a few minutes, houses from Quogue Village to Moriches Inlet were wiped out."

———

Pat Driver has been to many parties in her seventy-five years, but the one she remembers most vividly is the Greenes' end-of-summer party on Westhampton Beach when she was ten years old. "At first, the weather didn't stop the fun we were having," she recalled. "But as time went by, into the early afternoon, the storm increased and the noise of the wind became quite frightening."

Tot Greene grew apprehensive. As the afternoon turned nasty, she decided to ask the parents to pick up their children early. She was making the first call when the phone died. The electricity failed next. Then the wind tore off the garage doors, dropping them like a thunderclap in the driveway. Tot was supposed to meet her husband Norv at the train at 3:30 P.M., but now she could not get her car out.

While she was wondering how to pick up Norv and how to explain to him that their garage was wrecked, there was a pounding on the front door. The bell, like everything else electrical, was out, and at first Tot thought it was the wind knocking. As the sound persisted, she peered out.

A wet, windswept, clearly terrified group shivered on her doorstep. Tot counted ten: the young couple who lived in the oceanfront house across the street, their two crying babies and the babies' nursemaid, their cook and her husband, and three local movers who had been packing up the family for the move back to the city. The group had fled across Dune Road, with the Atlantic at their heels. The surf was breaking over the beach and flooding the houses on the ocean side. Along Westhampton Beach, the tide would rise as high as thirty feet.

Within a few minutes, waves were flattening the dunes and advancing on the Greenes' house. Pat Driver heard one of the grown-ups say, "'Don't let the children see.' Of course, we ran right to the windows and looked out, and at the awful sight, we all burst into tears. I will never in all my life forget the sight of the huge wave rolling over the dunes, coming right for us."

Within minutes, the ocean was banging on the Greenes' front door. It pounded on the windows and stormed in. Tot and her "houseguests" all fled to the second floor. Tot asked the men to each take a child in case the house fell, only to discover that none of them could swim. She could find only one life preserver. "I could not in all conscience give it to one of my children. Taking advantage of my indecision, ten-year-old Margaret Bradley grabbed it and put it on. 'Don't you think your little brother Otis should have it?' I asked. The answer was, 'No, girls first!'"

Waves crushed the Greenes' front staircase and washed away the living room wing and the master bedroom above it. The wing had been built on piles. The rest of the house and the garage were anchored in concrete. Tot watched her living room disappear. Parts of other Dune Road houses whizzed by, too, driven by a screaming wind. The sea smashed against what remained of the house as if demanding more. When it reached the second floor, the group escaped to the attic. The nursemaid began to wail, "We will all be drowned." Tot told her in no uncertain terms to pull herself together. She was frightening the children.

The Greenes' attic was dark and cramped. "It was a very small space for so many very frightened people," Pat Driver remembered. "Everyone was quiet, while the noise of the storm was terrible. We children, especially the younger ones, were in tears and sobbed continually. Someone said, 'We've done all we can; now all we can do is pray.' And so we did. I repeated over and over again the only prayer I knew, 'Now, I lay me down to sleep.' It seemed very inadequate to the situation.

"The scene around us in the attic was unbelievable. The waves, at the level of the attic floor, beat unceasingly against the house, which trembled and shook. It was as dark as night, and we all thought our last moment had come."

The men punched a hole in the roof. They thought the house would go at any moment, and when it collapsed, they could ride the roof over to the mainland. The plan was no sooner hatched than, to their horror, a similar roof from a nearby house collapsed and disappeared into Moriches Bay.

When the power went out on the South Shore of Long Island about 2:40 P.M., Dr. Leray Davis's Oldsmobile was suspended on the pneumatic lift at the local garage. Davis, one of the town's two doctors, borrowed his wife's Chevy to make house calls. But first, he swung by the local school, picked up his son, Lee, and dropped him off at home. Dr. Davis went in for a minute to check his barometer. It was a handsome instrument, shaped like a silver ship's wheel. He shook it, angry with Okey Overton, the local jeweler who had sold it to him. The indicator was frozen at the bottom of the scale in the area marked HURRICANE. Still annoyed, Dr. Davis left to make his calls.

Although he was only eight years old, Lee Davis remembers every detail of that afternoon from the moment his father drove away in the family's only functioning car: "Priorities have a way of arranging themselves along the rim of disaster. They did that day. The dog had disappeared. I couldn't decide which comic book to save. My mother was ordering me to put on my rubbers. By contrast, my grandmother, who the day before had just been released from the hospital, was as calm as a clearing in the woods, while my grandfather bundled her into her black Persian lamb coat."

The Davises lived in Westhampton Village, a block south of Main Street across from the country club. With no car, everyone in their household — eight-year-old Lee; his mother; his grandparents; two domestics, Minnie and Louis; and Lee's dog, Toby — set out on foot.

"My mother grabbed my free hand and pulled," Davis recalled, "and together we stumbled forward, bullying our way through the water that splashed against the stone steps of the house, gurgled in the cellar window wells, and seemed to be constantly, breathlessly in motion. The sky was still a grayish green, reflecting the water, and beyond it, bouncing off the surface of the sky, was the wind." The Davises reached the highway, with the Sound foaming behind them.

Two cars stopped. "The doors of both opened, and like gathering arms, drew in first my grandmother and then my grandfather and Minnie, then my mother and myself. By now the water was above the running board of the car. Holding a protesting Toby next to my chest, I piled into the back beside a thoroughly terrified woman. My mother climbed in after me. Louis reached for the outside handle of the passenger side of the front seat. The driver, a slight, immaculately dressed man with a sallow complexion, reached over and swiftly locked it. 'No niggers ride in this car,' he said calmly, and gunned the motor. The car skidded sideways, forcing Louis to leap backwards.

"'You can't do that,' my mother screamed. The driver glanced over his shoulder. 'You want to be with him? Get out.'

"My mother settled forlornly back in her seat. I twisted around and looked through the rear window at the second incredible scene of that day, one that would remain as vividly with me as if it happened within the last five minutes.

"Louis, his coat plastered closely to him from the driving rain, my father's best hat on his head, was running behind the car, waving his arms, yelling silently. The water was swirling around his ankles as he drew farther and farther behind the steadily accelerating car."

Sometime later, Dr. Davis was administering first aid to survivors. He looked across the street and saw Louis wandering through the wrecked village, wet and dazed. Lee Davis said, "My father was wondering why in hell Louis was there, and where in hell the family was, and why in hell Louis was wearing his best hat. Then the two of them set off on the heartbreaking task of tending to the wounded and gathering up the dead."

Many of the "colored help" who had been left behind to close up the summer estates did not know how to swim. In the toll of dead and missing published in local newspapers, the victims would be identified by name and color. At least one fleeing family piled into the car and left the help behind to fend for themselves. Others risked their lives to save them.

Mona and Joan Schmid were convent girls, graduates of Maplehurst and Manhattanville College of the Sacred Heart, the privileged daughters of a prominent Brooklyn attorney. In spite of the dismal weather on Wednesday, their mood was as light as the frothy Astaire-Rogers tune from *Top Hat*, "Isn't This a Lovely Day to Be Caught in the Rain."

Both girls were popular, but Mona was a beauty. She had small, delicate features, a peaches-and-cream complexion, and raven hair. The Schmids came to Westhampton every summer, staying from May through October. They rented a house nestled behind a high dune on the bay side.

"Life was quiet and fun," Mona remembers. "Nobody cared who anybody was. President Roosevelt was a frequent Westhampton visitor, but no one made a fuss." He stayed with his friend and former law partner Basil O'Connor. That same year, the two men organized the March of Dimes, the first charity radiothon. It raised millions for the fight against polio. Comedian Eddie Cantor, who emceed the show, coined the title "March of Dimes," playing off the famous "March of Time" newsreels. In a strange twist of fate, Basil O'Connor's daughter would contract polio, too.

Like so many others, the Schmid sisters thought the gusty Wednesday weather was normal. "Every September there was a three-day wind when the breakers would be spectacular," Mona remembered. "Friends called to ask if we'd like to go to the ocean to watch, but we refused because we had to visit Peggy." Peggy was Peggy Connolly Brown, the wife of a young attorney. The Browns lived in an oceanfront cottage about half a mile down Dune Road with their seven-month-old daughter, Judith. In the morning, Mona and Joan did some errands with Annie Seeley, their maid. Annie had worked for the Schmids for seventeen years. The sisters couldn't remember life without her. They arrived at Peggy's house about three o'clock. It was already very windy, and in a matter of minutes, a frantic call came from Annie. She was on the third floor. The ocean was on the second. While Joan was trying to reassure her, the phone died. Her call must have been one of the last to get through.

Afraid for Annie's safety, Mona and Joan started home. They were driving their mother's car, a gray and red Cadillac La Salle with her monogram on the side. Dune Road was flooded. As they crept through the rising water, a friend called from one of the houses, inviting them to come in out of the storm. "No thanks," the sisters shouted back, "we have to get home to Annie."

That proved impossible. A few minutes later the La Salle shorted. Thinking they could find shelter behind one of the high dunes, Mona and Joan left the car and started walking. "We got maybe thirty feet," Mona said, "when we realized we'd forgotten the keys in the ignition. We turned back to retrieve them. The car was gone. The wind picked up everything."

The Schmids found an old rowboat behind a dune and used it for shelter. They were crouching there when a long black car came down the road driven by a black chauffeur. With him were his sister and his employer, a paraplegic man. Their car stalled, too, and then there were five behind the dune. As luck would have it, a lone telephone pole was still standing near them. The chauffeur found two ropes. He looped one around the pole and then around his group. Mona and Joan refused to be tied down. Joan thought if they were free to swim, they would have a better chance of survival. The water loomed over the dune. "Everyone was praying. I was promising the good Lord everything," Mona said.

Scenes of devastation were repeated all along the South Shore of Long Island. At Quogue, Southampton, and Water Mill, the inland highway flooded, cutting off Montauk from the rest of the island. A Greenport man driving home from Manhattan was stopped in his tracks: "Where a well-paved state highway ordinarily lay, the Atlantic intervened in all its formidable majesty." In the village of Westhampton, a mile from shore, water rose to seven feet on Main Street. The Shinnecock Bay Coast Guard Station with its steel lookout tower and hundred-foot radio mast washed into the bay. The guardsmen just managed to reach their boats in time.

At Sag Harbor the great steeple of the Presbyterian church collapsed. The church was more than a hundred feet tall and almost a hundred years old. For generations, a light had always burned in the steeple to guide Long Island whalers and fishermen home from the sea. When the steeple fell, it brought down a tradition that had lasted for decades. In Southampton the beautiful Dune Church was demolished, except for the east wall, inscribed with the biblical quotation "Thou rulest the raging of the sea. Thou stillest the waves thereof when they arise."

CHAPTER 13

Crossing the Sound

Long Island absorbed the first shock of the storm. The long
arm that stretches a hundred miles northeastward from New
York City acted like an enormous breakwater, protecting most of
coastal Connecticut from the worst onslaught. Only the very
easterly Connecticut towns, from Old Saybrook to Stonington,
and all of Rhode Island faced the open ocean unguarded.

Although it is the rare hurricane that arrives so far north at
maximum strength, the few that make it are engines of enormous
speed and power. Gordon Dunn called them "the most destructive hurricanes of record since the Pilgrims landed at Plymouth
Rock." In the sodden September of 1938, New England was a
hothouse. The prevailing conditions — high humidity, ocean
waters as warm as a bath, and saturated terrain — were a hurricane's favorite weather, and so it passed from one steam heat to
another, replenishing itself as it rushed north.

Landfall usually acts like a brake. A hurricane moves unop-
posed across the smooth ocean surface because there is nothing

to impede its progress. Once the storm reaches land, however, it encounters friction, the force created when one surface tries to move across another. The rougher land terrain, with its myriad obstacles — trees, hills, dunes, buildings — slows and flattens its progress. After traveling over land for 150 miles, a cyclone's strength and speed are usually cut in half.

Not this time. Gaining rather than losing intensity, the Great Hurricane of 1938 swooped across Long Island Sound and smacked New England. Mountains, valleys, urban sprawl — nothing stopped it. The hurricane was more terrible than anything New England had ever experienced. By four o'clock, the worst winds in a hundred years were battering colonial villages. They cut off power, leaving most of New England in darkness, and toppled weather towers built to gauge it. Great elms and oaks as old as the nation leaned into the wind and lay down. One by one, beautiful lindens and willows fell. The ground was so wet that the wind yanked the ancient trees out, roots and all. By the end of the day, picturesque village greens and lovely Ivy League campuses looked like logging camps.

At Wesleyan, in Middletown, Connecticut, minutes after the opening exercises for the new school term concluded, the old stone tower of the chapel blew down. At Tabor Academy, an exclusive prep school on the Massachusetts shore, there was no sign that unusual weather was on the way until half past two. A Tabor teacher described "black, ominous-looking rolls of rain-laden clouds that came up out of the southeast driven by fast-driving winds. By four o'clock the storm was over the school in full, unimagined fury." The Tabor gym became a swimming pool, and teachers ferried the boys between buildings in racing shells. The water was so high, they tied up at the second floor, and the boys crawled through the windows into their dormitories.

The main house and barns of Fox Hill Farm

Three of the Matoes children:
Theresa, Joseph Jr., and Dorothy
Courtesy of Patricia M. Vandal

The Chellises'
Beavertail
Lighthouse home

Clayton Chellis

Marion Chellis

The Moore children in 1935 or 1936: Anne, Cathy, Margaret, and Geoffrey Jr.

The Moores' Fort Road beach house, taken from their dock
on Little Narragansett Bay. The Nestors' house is to the right.

Jeff and Catherine Moore

Andy Pupillo,
who worked for the Moores

Ocean spumes shot up like geysers, creating a wall of water as high as fifty feet along New England's southern coast.
NOAA Photo Library

Satellite View: Seen from space, a hurricane looks like a swirl of marshmallow frosting. The dot in the center is the eye of the storm.
NOAA Photo Library

The hurricane reaches the South County coast of Rhode Island.
NOAA Photo Library

Stunned Long Islanders
survey what remained of Westhampton Beach.

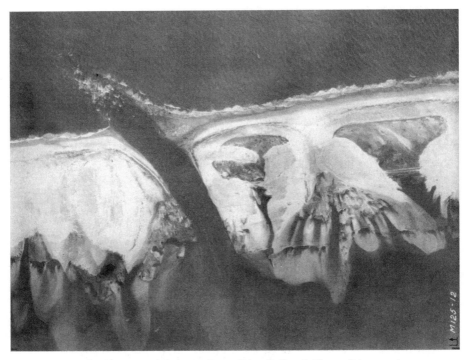

The Shinnecock Inlet on Long Island's South Shore did not exist
until the 1938 hurricane breached the barrier island.
Beach Erosion Board Archives

Westhampton Beach lost 153 houses, and like this beachfront mansion,
most of those remaining were shells.
Courtesy of Gretchen Greene Royce

Patricia Driver, one of the children at
the Greenes' Westhampton Beach party

The Greenes' home, beaten but still standing
Courtesy of Gretchen Greene Royce

Some houses — like this one in Stonington — were simply upended.
Hurricane Collection of George H. Utter, Westerly, R.I.

Katharine Hepburn played her
best game of golf, shooting a hole
in one on the ninth hole of
the Fenwick golf course,
the morning of the hurricane.

Somewhere between Mystic and Stonington,
the storm derailed the *Bostonian*, the 11 A.M.
Shore Line Limited,
from New York to Boston.

The 10,000-ton lighthouse tender *Tulip* interrupted train service on the New York, New Haven & Hartford line — and that was the least of New London's woes.
both Courtesy of www.railroadextra.com

Wind, water, and fire devastated the city's waterfront.

Car roofs looked like stepping-stones in the swirling water that turned downtown Providence, R.I., into a lake, seventeen feet at its deepest point.

Fort Road, Napatree, as seen from Watch Hill.
(The Watch Hill Beach Club is in the forefront, the Geoffrey Moore house
is the big, light-colored one toward the point.)
Hurricane Collection of George H. Utter, Westerly, R.I.

Napatree from the same spot, a day later
Hurricane Collection of George H. Utter, Westerly, R.I.

The road to nowhere at Island Park, Portsmouth, a beach community
on the north end of Aquidneck Island. Nineteen died in Island Park.
NOAA Photo Library

All of Newport's exclusive
Bailey's Beach washed away,
except this central section.
*R.I. Collection
at Providence Public Library*

A chimney stands like a lone sentinel,
the only vestige of a Newport beach house.
NOAA Photo Library

The beach pavilion at Mackerel Cove, Jamestown,
had 100 cabanas on the first floor and a ballroom upstairs.
Collection of Jamestown, R.I., Historical Society

All that remained of the beach pavilion were the stone steps.
Collection of Jamestown, R.I., Historical Society

In the western Massachusetts town of Ware, the river rampaged down
Main Street, rushing by a bridge that had spanned it hours before.
NOAA Photo Library

The hurricane sea breaking over Woods Hole, Massachusetts
NOAA Photo Library

New Bedford: A NO TRESPASSING sign did not deter the hurricane.
Desolate owners sit in the remnants of their home.
NOAA Photo Library

Buzzards Bay: Wind and water flattened a beach community
at the mouth of the Cape Cod Canal.
NOAA Photo Library

Winds uprooted ancient trees — like this one that crushed a car in Hartford, Connecticut. *National Archives*

Like New London, Peterborough, New Hampshire, was ravaged by wind, floods, and fire. *Peterborough, N.H., Historical Society*

At Manchester, the Merrimack River stood at full flood after the hurricane. *NOAA Photo Library*

The Jamestown school bus, abandoned and half submerged
in the muck of Sheffield Cove
Collection of Jamestown, R.I., Historical Society

Entire beach communities were lost.
This broken shell of Pleasant View
House, a large oceanfront hotel,
was just about all that was left
of Misquamicut, R.I.
National Archives

Teetering on a mound of sand, this
Rhode Island beach house was salvaged
and still stands today.
Hurricane Collection of George H. Utter, Westerly, R.I.

Clayton Chellis *(second from left)* in 1945 on his last
home leave with his parents, Carl *(left)* and Ethel,
and his brother, Bill

Lillian and Jack Kinney, fifty
years later. After surviving
the hurricane in the old
Napatree fort, they believed
that, together, they could
survive anything.
*Hurricane Collection of
George H. Utter, Westerly, R.I.*

The morning after, the southern New England shoreline
looked like a huge yard sale.
Hurricane Collection of George H. Utter, Westerly, R.I.

Boats were everywhere except at their
moorings. They were beached on main
streets and in backyards.

So many trees fell, there was
enough timber to build 200,000
five-room houses. Sawing and
salvaging it would take five years.
*both Hurricane Collection of
George H. Utter, Westerly, R.I.*

At Northfield Seminary, a girls' boarding school in Massachusetts, a chimney crashed through the ceiling of the dining hall, killing two girls as they ate supper. At Amherst College, Dean Harry N. Glick reported that an otherwise unexceptional group of freshmen taking an IQ test that afternoon scored higher than any class, before or since.

In a satellite photograph, a hurricane appears uniform. No one area looks much different from another. But within the same storm, there are enormous differences and degrees of ferocity. The center, or eye, of the storm is a circle of tranquillity and blue sky, typically forty or fifty miles in diameter. In the relatively tame outer rim, winds may be as weak as thirty or forty miles per hour, strong enough to be disruptive but not disastrous. The terror comes in between, from the eyewall, a swirl of violent thunderstorms and screaming winds surrounding the eye. The heaviest rain falls to the west of the eyewall; the highest winds blow to the east in the area called the dangerous right semicircle. There is no worse place to be. In the Northern Hemisphere, winds blow counterclockwise because of the way the earth spins; so, east of the eye, internal winds are whirling in the same direction as the storm is moving. There, in the dangerous right semicircle, combined winds may be as wild as two hundred miles per hour — sudden destruction when encountered.

The eye of the storm passed over Connecticut between Bridgeport and New Haven in the late afternoon, then swept through New England just west of Hartford and roughly equidistant from New York and Boston. The relatively tame outer rim brushed both cities. In Boston the Braves had just lost the first game of a doubleheader to the St. Louis Cardinals. They were starting the second when the hurricane swiped at the city. It could not have come at a more opportune moment for Vince DiMaggio. In the eighth inning of the first game, DiMaggio had fanned on a fastball from Paul Dean, Dizzy Dean's kid brother, to tie the National League record for most strikeouts — 113. DiMaggio struck out again at the start of the second game. He was going to make the record books when the game was called.

Down at the Boston Navy Yard, "Old Ironsides" was torn from her anchorage and pummeled. Out at the Boston airport, seventy-five miles from the center of the storm, gale winds knocked down a one-hundred-foot radio tower, cutting off all air-to-ground communications, then picked up an eight-ton American Airlines DC-2, flung it across the runway, and dropped it in a salt marsh half a mile away.

Rains from the western side of the eyewall drenched the already waterlogged Connecticut River Valley and western Massachusetts, causing record flooding. One inch of rainfall on an acre of land drops 113 tons of water. Up to seventeen inches — more than 19,000 tons — had fallen on Connecticut and Massachusetts in five days. If the rain had been snow, New England would have been buried under ten feet. Rivers already swollen from weeks of thunderstorms crested. In Hartford, the Connecticut River rose 19.4 feet above flood stage, to 35.4 feet. The Deerfield River rose more than 20 feet. Thousands of volunteers formed assembly lines, piling the riverbanks with sandbags against the rising waters.

Hurricane winds roared through the tobacco farms of the Connecticut River Valley and the mill towns of central Massachusetts, where rivers were already at perilous heights. Placid streams became rushing rivers. Floodwaters washed away roadways and railways. Valley towns were cut off. The rivers that had made New England a vital manufacturing center swept through the mill towns and crushed them. In Norwich, the Thames rose seven feet in one hour and rushed south, carrying the spoils of upstream mill towns. In Ware, a town of fewer than eight thousand, the storm rerouted the normally meandering river. It coursed down Main Street, splitting the village in two. Groceries and mail had to be delivered in baskets strung across the street on pulleys. The floodwater peaked at a record 18.2 feet; when it receded, all that was left of Main Street were the sewer pipes. In Worcester, two old brick factories crumbled under the assault of wind and water.

Under the cover of night, the hurricane sped through the Berkshires. It knocked down 16,000 hardwood trees in Springfield, Massachusetts; sliced down the maple woods of Vermont; and screeched across the White Mountains of New Hampshire. On Mount Washington, where Jacob's Ladder on the scenic cog railroad was demolished, winds were clocked at more than a hundred miles per hour.

In New Hampshire, floods and fire turned Peterborough into a charred ruin. When the Contoocook River flooded the business district, electric circuits were shorted and the town's biggest employers, the Transcript Printing Company and the Farmer's Grain Company, burned. Fanned by gale winds, flames rushed down Main Street and spread to the neighboring forest. In Weare, located near Concord, the Piscataquog River raced through town after two upstream reservoirs burst. Four women who were standing on a bridge watching the unruly river drowned when the bridge collapsed. In all, thirteen died and 6,000 were left homeless in New Hampshire.

By eight o'clock Wednesday night, Vermont was feeling the hurricane's might. A husband and wife were enjoying a leisurely dinner in their prefabricated vacation house in the Green Mountains when the lights went out. The roof and walls blew away, never to be found again. The couple finished their dinner alfresco. The hurricane veered west around Burlington and bombarded upstate New Yorkers while they slept. It raised the waters of Lake Champlain, which is 435 square miles, by two feet.

Along the coast, the Cape Cod Canal, which cuts a channel from Buzzards Bay to the ocean, saved much of Massachusetts' shore from the full fury of the storm. When the tide rose to almost sixteen feet, the canal provided an outlet for the water. It also protected the long hook of Cape Cod. Safeguarded on its inland side by the canal and on the ocean side by steep clay cliffs, the Cape escaped New England's worst hurricane with little more than a glancing blow.

In New England the full rip of the storm was reserved for the southern shore of Massachusetts, the easternmost beach towns of Connecticut, and all of coastal Rhode Island. There, the ferocity of the storm surpassed even the Great September Gale of 1815 and the legendary Colonial Hurricane of 1635, which the Pilgrims believed was apocalyptic.

CHAPTER 14

The Atlantic Ocean Bound Out of Bed

I f you blow across a strip of paper, the end will flutter and rise. If you blow harder, the paper will crackle and snap. The same basic law of physics is at work in a hurricane. When a cyclone blusters in from the ocean, it roils the water beneath it. The stronger the winds, the angrier the sea becomes. In the dangerous right semicircle, where the winds are fiercest, the sea is driven with tremendous speed, creating a huge swell of water known as a storm surge.

Meteorologists do not fully understand this phenomenon, but a storm surge may be shaped like a dome, a wall, or a series of enormous waves. A rapid rise in sea level occurs along a shoreline as the eye of the storm makes landfall. The winds propel the sea with such velocity that one wave does not have time to ebb before the next one rushes in. The waves pile up on top of one another, like snow pushed before a plow, and tens of thousands of tons of water crash over the shore.

Like a tsunami, a storm surge is sudden and lethal, especially if it coincides with a high tide. The height of the surge is superimposed on the natural tide, causing a titanic rise that rips loose everything in its path. Within it, acres of debris spin in a furious whirl. Hurricane winds alone are ferocious, but the menace from a storm surge is a thousand times worse. It causes three-fourths of all hurricane deaths.

Sometime near three o'clock, from Old Saybrook, Connecticut, to Buzzards Bay, Massachusetts, the sea began to stir. The water came in slowly at first, encroaching on the shore, slithering up beyond the highest high-water mark. It seeped under pilings and oozed through floorboards. Water was everywhere, in places it had never been and could not have reached moments before. While pools of water were gathering in unexpected places, suddenly, to the amazement and disbelief of all who witnessed it, the Atlantic Ocean rose from the bed where it had lain for one hundred years and came ashore. Those who saw the tower of water rising over the sand did not believe what they were seeing. They thought it was a bank of fog, a trick of the storm, a mirage.

The last time the Atlantic had leapt from its bed was in the Great September Gale of 1815. In the intervening century, as the nation expanded and prospered, the lesson of history was forgotten. By 1938, the barrier beaches of Long Island and southern New England, with their panoramic views and dramatic dunes, had become popular summer resorts crowded with houses — all kinds of houses, from fishing shacks and modest bungalows to shingled cottages and beachfront mansions.

When the hurricane's dangerous right semicircle reached these shores, the storm surge swept over the low-lying beaches and squeezed into the bays. On Buzzards Bay, it picked up an eight-room house and sent it somersaulting down the sand, with the family still inside. As the house turned over and over, father, mother, and children were tumbled like a load of clothes in a washing machine. They were bruised black and blue and battered to death.

In Connecticut, the storm surge menaced coastal towns lying in the seventy-mile stretch of shoreline beyond the shelter of Long Island. It inundated Fenwick, Mystic, and Stonington, where the wary Portuguese fishermen had stayed in port. Caution saved their lives but not their livelihood. The Stonington fishing fleet numbered fifty-two boats. Fifty were sunk or smashed beyond repair.

In Fenwick, Katharine Hepburn came out of the water after her afternoon swim to a hail of stinging sand. The wind was so strong that when she leaned against it, it held her up. The wild, whitecapped Sound was thrilling, and she had stayed in longer than usual, riding the tremendous breakers.

Although the Hepburns' house was just steps from the water, by the time she reached it, the tide was rolling over the bulkhead and breaking across the lawn. The rain, which had been a fine mist when she was swimming, was coming down in torrents. In rapid succession, a car parked in the driveway flew though the air, two chimneys collapsed, and windows shattered, blown out on one side of the house, sucked in on the other. Water rushed through the first floor.

"After that second swim we began to realize that we were in for something special," Hepburn would write in her autobiography. "The screens on the porch began to blow like a lady's petticoat. Then there was a rip and a crash and the big laundry wing fell off the back of the house. By this time the wind seemed to have doubled its strength."

In New London the *Bostonian* finally eased out of the station at about four o'clock and crawled toward Mystic at twenty miles an hour. A few miles east of the station it bumped against the fury of the storm and stopped in its tracks. Between Mystic and Stonington the railway is laid out along a narrow causeway built on a bed of boulders and crushed gravel. The September rains had undermined the bed and weakened the trestle.

As the Shore Line Limited started across the causeway, breaking waves were rolling toward the tracks and debris was smashing against the cars. Engineer Harry Easton cut his speed "to the pace of a slug." He was halfway across and proceeding "with extreme caution" when a red signal flashed from the control tower ahead. The *Bostonian* skidded to a halt. The middle of a narrow exposed trestle was the worst possible place to stop in a gale. The sea was rising on one side, and a normally placid salt pond was bubbling like a geyser on the other. Easton wanted permission to continue across.

He climbed down from the engine and walked along the track to the tower — just a short distance, maybe two city blocks. The water was licking the tracks when he set out. By the time he started back to the train, it was up to his ankles. A few more steps and it was up to his knees. "You can get some idea how fast that water came up from the fact that we started running and before we got to the engine, the water was up to our hips." The Pullman cars, each weighing sixty-seven tons, were swaying like the top seats of a Ferris wheel. Wind and water rose higher and higher.

Sealed in the capsule of glass and metal, the passengers waited with varying degrees of impatience but no real sense of alarm, until the windows began to go. One after another on the seaward side, they cracked or popped out and shattered. Glass shards and water flew into the cars, and the coaches began to list toward the sea. Conductor Joe Richards went through, asking passengers to move to the inland side of the train to avoid injury. Caught on the exposed coastline between Mystic and Stonington, unable to help themselves, they waited in the teeth of the hurricane for what seemed an eternity.

The flying glass was frightening, but a much greater danger was unseen. Beneath the tracks, the railbed was disappearing. By 4:30 P.M., the posh parlor car Oriental was dangling over an abyss. Only its front wheels still held the track. There were no rails, no ties, and no bed left beneath it. Easton and Richards decided that their only chance was to crowd everyone into the front cars, cut off the others, and make a run for the station house in Stonington.

The conductor walked through the car again, ordering all passengers to move up to the front of the train. A few required firmer action. When some of the prep school boys clowned around, ignoring his orders, Richards ripped open an emergency case, pulled out the axe, and threatened them with it. One couple was in the middle of dinner. Although the dining car was tilting dangerously, the diners objected to having their meal interrupted. They had paid for it, and they insisted on finishing it.

To prevent panic, the stewards continued setting fresh tables, shaking out crisp cloths and laying the silverware as if nothing were wrong. The ruse failed. Instead of an orderly line advancing to the front of the train, frightened passengers and porters poured into the aisles. Some began to shove. Others deserted the train and tried to swim to safety. Still others, in their rush to reach the front cars, got off the train. Hugging the wheels of the cars, they slogged through the surging water.

Engineer Easton saw people "leaping in terror from windows, doors and platforms into the water." The train crew yelled to them to get back inside and forced all the passengers forward. They squeezed as many women and children as possible into the engine car. The rest were packed into the front car or took their chances in the churning water.

Seventeen-year-old Elvine Richard and her mother threw their coats, hats, and pocketbooks into the whirlpool and jumped. A terrifying undertow dragged them down. Broken branches, broken houses, broken boats, swirled in the water. Many of those engulfed by the storm were beaten to death by the wreckage. When a tree branch slammed into Elvine, fracturing her leg, two boys pulled her through the water — Stephen Glidden, a sixteen-year-old prep school boy, and Edward Brown, an MIT student. A burly passenger took a three-year-old boy from his struggling mother's arms and started to carry him through the waist-high water. "Biting spray lashed our faces and surging waves tugged at our legs," she remembered. The man lost his footing and fell into the water with her baby. Easton saw him stumble and went to their rescue. A wave caught one of the Fessenden boys; Roderick Hagenbuckle hauled him back. Once they realized that the peril was real, the boys helped many to safety.

Ed Flanagan, the Democratic Party chairman from Providence, described the exodus: "We got as far as the trestle west of Stonington, where the water was hurling boats and houses up against the side of the train. The roof of a house crashed into the side of the dining car. As the water began to beat against the train, we were ordered off. We walked the trestle up to the locomotive but could get no farther because of the rush of water. Passengers clung to the cables and engine wheels. Some of them were finally swept away. I saw them go with my own eyes."

Passengers squashed into the engine, hung on to the tender, crammed into the first car. Lawrence Burwell, the Brown University senior, was packed in with some 175 others. No one could move forward or back.

We waited breathlessly for the rapidly rising tide to engulf the coach completely. Waves ten feet and higher pounded through the windows. We could hear the locomotive attempting to struggle forward to higher ground, its whistle screeching as if in defiance to the maelstrom around us. Baggage could be seen floating in every direction. People were trying to climb into the baggage racks thinking that this would be the least vulnerable point. The tracks had now so completely given way that the cars shook and some, in falling, broke away from the only two left standing upright.

Through the shattered train window, Burwell saw a woman with two young children in the second story of a house. The house was floating on the water. One wall had been torn away, leaving the interior exposed like a dollhouse. Mother and children clung together. As Burwell watched, "a terrific blast ripped off the roof. The walls fell apart, the flooring gave way, and the woman and children plunged into the heaving sea of wreckage." He said, "No experience, no matter how harrowing, could compare with the tragedy enacted before those of us who were forced to look on helpless."

Two more Pullman cars were swept from the rails. It seemed just a matter of minutes before the *Bostonian* would be sucked in after them. The railbed was eroding rapidly. As if the situation were not precarious enough, a big timber hit the train's air hose and the emergency brakes jammed. The *Bostonian* was locked in place with its empty cars hanging off the edge of the track. If they toppled, they would pull the entire train into the abyss of water.

Back in New London, the city they had just left, the lighthouse tender, *Tulip,* 190 feet long and weighing more than ten thousand tons, was lifted out of the harbor and was carried across the rail-road tracks. She sat in the center of town, straddling the east-bound tracks of the New Haven Railroad for seventeen days. Relaunching her would be an engineering feat — and that was the least of New London's woes. Crackling power lines and furi-ous winds turned the downtown district into an inferno. The city burned for the second time in its history. (The first fire was set by Benedict Arnold to halt the British advance.)

Bernie Kenyon and his friends were catching a Wednesday matinee in downtown New London when the film sputtered and the screen went blank. Kenyon doesn't recall the movie, but he remembers very well stepping out of the theater and being nabbed by the police. "Every able-bodied man in town was recruited to battle the blaze." Hurricane winds fanned the fire. The flames shot from block to block through the downtown dis-trict. Burning cinders carried on the wind ignited random houses miles away. Power outages reduced the flow of water to a trickle. Water was everywhere except in the hoses, which were running dry. Fire engines from neighboring towns were blocked by forests of fallen trees. For six hours New London burned unchecked. "We thought the whole city was going," Kenyon said. But the winds changed as the storm moved north, shifting from southeast to southwest, and the fire turned in on itself.

The *Bostonian* was an island, surrounded by churning, debris-filled water more than five feet deep. Uncoupling the front cars seemed an almost impossible feat, but brakeman Bill Donoghue plunged into the water. First he had to turn off the air compressor so the train could build up enough pressure to start again, then he had to uncouple the engine, tender, and first car from the rest of the train. If he failed, the *Bostonian* was doomed. Lashed by the vicious wind, beaten by the flotsam that filled the water, Donoghue worked against the powerful undertow. After several futile attempts, he finally managed to shut off the compressor and pull the pin. By then, too exhausted to save himself, he floated belly-up; Joe Richards hung out of the train, grabbed him, and dragged him in.

Whistle blasting, the abbreviated *Bostonian* tried to make a getaway. Three times the wheels failed to grip the track. On the fourth try, Easton opened the throttle all the way. Like the little engine that could, Engine No. 14 bolted and groaned, then began to move slowly. With women and children "clustered like flies" on the engine and the desperate passengers cheering, Easton nudged aside a telephone pole, two fishing boats, and a house that had washed up onto the tracks. A light rowboat drifted across the rails. The *Bostonian* "cracked it like a shell." Dragging telegraph wires and poles, it inched safely down the track and arrived at Stonington.

Easton described the final miles for *Railroad* magazine:

Crates, logs and small boats kept smashing against our locomotive. Just as I thought the worst might be over, something heavy thumped the front end. A full-sized sail-boat, tilted to one side, was lodged on the track. Slowly our wheels ground forward. The boat was firmly wedged. My hand could feel the deep vibration as the engine's power drove against the heavy barrier of wood. We were stopped now, maybe for the last time. Then something snapped. The craft revolved sickly, turned bottom up, and began bumping rapidly for shore. Roaring her triumph, the big engine nosed ashore. When I looked back I could see sparks streaming from the wheels but I kept right onto the crossing near the station before I stopped and thanked God we were safe.

When the *Bostonian* reached Stonington, passengers and crew were brought to the Catholic church, where they received food, dry clothes, and a place to sleep. They were bused to Providence and Boston the next day. Students arrived at Harvard and Brown dressed in dungarees and engineer caps, without a stitch of clothes except what they were wearing. The Ivy League colleges extended their registration period through the week. Many students formed volunteer corps and aided the relief workers.

There were only two *Bostonian* fatalities. Bertha Weinstein Markell of Hartford, a passenger who was described as "an elderly well-dressed woman," jumped into the swelling water and disappeared. Chester A. Walker, a pantryman, was also killed. Whether he panicked and died trying to escape from the stranded cars or whether he was killed trying to save Bertha Markell is not known. According to the conductor, a piece of timber hit Walker in the back of the head. "He went down and never came up." Sometime later, his body was found in the garden of a house in Stonington.

In Fenwick, Katharine Hepburn was trapped inside the house with her mother, brother, a family friend, and the cook. The five tied themselves together with a rope and climbed through a dining room window. They dropped into waist-deep water. Like Scarlett escaping Atlanta, Hepburn battled her way to safety. "I slogged and sloshed, crawled through ditches and hung on to keep going somehow — got drenched and bruised and scratched."

When the Hepburns reached high ground, they looked back. Kate's Tara, which had endured tide and wind since the 1870s, pirouetted slowly and sailed away. "It went so quietly and in such a dignified manner, it seemed to be taking its afternoon stroll," Hepburn remembered. "It just sailed away easy as pie and soon there was nothing at all left. Our house — ours for twenty-five years — all our possessions — just gone. My God, it was something devastating and unreal, like the beginning of the world — or the end of it."

The day after the storm, Hepburn and her brother Dick returned to the beach. Digging in the sand where their home had stood for decades, they uncovered the complete set of their mother's flatware and her silver tea service.

Hepburn's affair with Howard Hughes did not fare as well as the family silver. Kate realized their romance was over when Hughes sent a planeload of fresh water instead of flying to Connecticut himself. In her autobiography, she described the end this way: "Love had turned to water. Pure water. But water. I think we really liked each other, but somehow — God sent the Hurricane of 1938." Eventually, Hepburn returned to Hollywood and lived for several years in a cottage on Hughes's estate. He orchestrated her movie comeback, insisting on a stellar supporting cast for the film version of *The Philadelphia Story*.

After his round-the-world flight, Hughes never attempted to set any other aviation records. His idiosyncrasies gradually came to dominate his life. The Hepburns rebuilt on the exact spot in Fenwick — a larger, grander house, which the actress and her brother have shared ever since.

CHAPTER 15

The Dangerous Right Semicircle

S urvivors in eastern Connecticut and Massachusetts could not believe that the storm was holding anything back, but the Hurricane of 1938 saved the worst for the smallest state. Although Rhode Island is just thirty-seven miles east to west and forty-eight miles north to south, its long shoreline and geography of deep bays and low barrier beaches made it uniquely vulnerable. The Ocean State not only lay directly in the path of the hurricane's dangerous right semicircle, it received the worst of the hurricane at the worst possible time — when the highest tide of the year was peaking.

Since colonial times, Rhode Islanders have marched to their own drummer, proudly, often defiantly. Rhode Island was the first colony to declare its independence and the last to ratify the Constitution. An adamant holdout for three years, it joined the other states only grudgingly. Rhode Islanders insist on their own clam

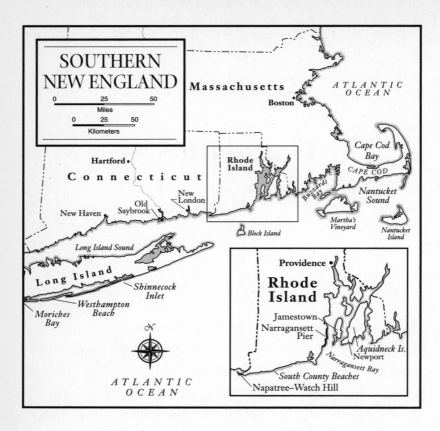

chowder made with quahogs (it is neither creamy nor red, but steeped in its natural broth); their own hot dogs, called Saugy's; and favorite local concoctions, jonnycakes and clam cakes, that didn't travel well over the state line. Rhode Islanders dunk french fries in vinegar (not ketchup) and drink coffee milk made with home-brewed syrup (Autocrat or Eclipse, now the same company) instead of chocolate milk. It goes without saying that if it's local, it's the best in the world. Rhode Islanders even have their own vocabulary. They order *cabinets* instead of *frappes* or *milk shakes;* serve *dropped eggs,* not *poached;* and drink from *bubblers,* not *water coolers. Wicked,* a favorite descriptive word way before it became hip, punctuates every second sentence.

Outsiders are apt to cite the state's size as the reason for so much contrariness, self-assertion as compensation for its small-ness — it would take five hundred Little Rhodys to fill Alaska — but Rhode Islanders know better. They come by their orneriness honestly. It is the legacy of Roger Williams, the state's founding father. "Prudence and principle" was his motto — and he lived by the latter half of it.

A charismatic Welshman, Oxford graduate, and ordained min-ister in the Church of England, Williams arrived in the New World aboard the frigate *Lyon* in 1631, just in time for the first Thanksgiving. He settled in the Puritan colony of Massachusetts Bay, where he was initially described as "a godly and zealous young minister." But Williams was a freethinker moving into a tight little theocratic community that prized conformity above all virtues. From the moment he set foot in the colonies, he was out of step.

From all reports, Williams was a popular pastor. His rolling Welsh voice, his total conviction, and his intellectual daring attracted many to his sermons, but his radical notions did not en-dear him to the Puritan elders. Williams preached absolute free-dom of conscience and religion. Thought, word, and action were rigorously controlled in the colonies, and few others dared whis-per such radical opinions, let alone shout them from the rooftops.

Within two months of his arrival, the censorious Pilgrim elders had Williams on their blacklist. Although he was a thorn in their side and a cause of considerable alarm, he managed to escape banishment for several years by shuttling between Massa-chusetts Bay and the slightly more tolerant colony of Plymouth. Whenever a crackdown seemed imminent, he went off and lived with the Indians to learn their language. Besides an open mind, Williams's greatest gift was a flair for languages. At Oxford, he had learned Latin, Greek, Hebrew, and several modern languages, and he applied his natural gift to mastering the native tongues. Since the Puritans considered the Indians "heathens and enemies of the Lord," such an eccentric ambition was further cause for scandal.

In 1635 Williams was branded a dangerous heretic and banished from the colonies. The General Court dispatched an unsavory captain named Underhill to seize the young preacher and deliver him to the first ship bound for England. Word of the deportation order spread swiftly, and before Underhill could act, Williams vanished. Except for a fort at Old Saybrook (in present-day Connecticut) to the south and an outpost at Portsmouth (now New Hampshire) to the north, Boston and Plymouth stood alone in a "pathless, dangerous wilderness." The colonies were surrounded on three sides by primeval forests that stretched inland with no apparent end. On the fourth lay the mercurial Atlantic. "I was sorely tossed for fourteen weeks in a bitter winter season, not knowing what bread or bed did mean," Williams wrote.

At that time, the Narragansett Indians were the most powerful tribe in the area that would become southern New England. They controlled the territory from Narragansett Bay in the east to the Pawcatuck River, now the boundary of Rhode Island and Connecticut, in the west. The Narragansetts rescued the exuberant preacher who spoke their tongue and brought no army. Their revered elder sachem Canonicus gave him land, protection, and grain to plant. By spring, Williams had thumbed his nose at his detractors and formed his own government-in-exile at the head of Narragansett Bay.

Of great personal charm and unquestioned integrity, Williams was liked and admired even by those, such as Massachusetts' governor John Winthrop, who abhorred his liberal ideas. Word of his democratic anchorage where church and state were separate and even Indians enjoyed freedom of thought, speech, and conscience attracted both disaffected Puritans and new settlers from England. The oldest American synagogue is located in Newport. By 1644, when Williams obtained a royal charter, the colony had four towns, two (Providence and Warwick) in the Providence Plantations and two (Portsmouth and Newport) on Aquidneck Island, the "isle of peace" at the mouth of the bay.

A large wishbone-shaped estuary scooped out millennia before by a glacier, Narragansett Bay was a prime location for a settlement. The largest bay in New England, it is thirty miles long and anywhere from three to twelve miles wide. Its rocky shores offered magnificent sites for homes, and the fields beyond had rich soil for orchards and crops. In 1664 a royal commission rated Narragansett Bay "the largest and safest port in New England, nearest to the sea and fittest for trade." Rhode Island soon became known as the "Garden of New England." It must have been galling for the Puritans to watch a colony built on such ungodly sentiments fatten and prosper.

As the colonial trade grew, the bay's natural inlets provided harbors for shipping, commerce, and skullduggery. Privateers and smugglers, including the infamous Captain Kidd, hid in its coves to surprise the clipper ships from Newport and Providence. Much of Rhode Island's old Yankee money was amassed by clipper ship captains who made their fortunes in the China trade, bartering opium for tea and blue Canton, while back home in the safe harbor of Providence, their families sank deep roots into the green hillsides.

By the time Rhode Island had grown to its full, if diminutive, size, it had a 420-mile coastline, anchored at either end by a bay. To the east is Narragansett Bay, with Providence at its head and the islands of Newport and Jamestown protecting its entrance. To the west is slipper-shaped Little Narragansett Bay, with

Watch Hill and Napatree. Between the two bays, from Watch Hill to Point Judith, lie a handful of seaside towns, strung along a twenty-mile stretch of coast known as South County. This is barrier beach land — low-lying strands of sand and dunes with a mix of Indian and Anglo names: Matunuck, Green Hill, Charlestown, Quonochontaug, Misquamicut, and Weekapaug. A series of similar beaches extends from southeastern Rhode Island into Buzzards Bay.

Barrier beaches are spits of shifting sands between two bodies of water, the sea on one side, lagoons and salt ponds on the other. The ocean builds the barrier beaches, and like an artist whose creation is never as perfect as the picture in his head, the sea continually sculpts and resculpts them. Pounding surf and ocean winds shape them, filling in the tidal flats with sloping dunes and dramatic bluffs, some as high as twenty feet. If you build on a barrier beach, you are toying with Nature. It is borrowed land on loan from the sea, and eventually, inevitably, the sea will come back to claim it. When a tropical intruder unexpectedly blows in, there is no more vulnerable place. Barrier beaches form a buffer zone of sorts between the ocean and the mainland. In a hurricane, they become killing fields.

The Great New England Hurricane of 1938 struck Rhode Island with a storm surge of unimagined dimensions. Like a barbarous army, it plundered the coast, gouging out beaches, leveling dunes, and rolling over bluffs, and when it had finished destroying its own handiwork, it took on human constructions. The ocean banged on doors and windows and burst through walls. It swirled into first-floor rooms and knocked down walls and stairways. Then it went upstairs into the bedrooms where families sought refuge, and chased them higher yet, into third floors and attics, onto rooftops, until there was no place to go but into the sea.

The density and force of water is a thousand times more powerful than the force of air. Under the double whammy of wind and wave, homes that had sheltered generations and weathered years of September gales folded as if they were built of cards. The sea swallowed some houses whole and smashed others to smithereens. Still others it lifted as carefully as a housewife rearranging the living room furniture and set down at a different place, sometimes a mile or more away, without splashing the milk in the creamer.

The suddenness of the storm surge was startling. Propelled by the furious wind, it came at such a speed that a man sixty feet from his front door and running all-out just made it into the house. Beach residents moved fast, but the sea moved faster. What to wear? What to bring? If they took time to pack an overnight bag, grab a toothbrush or a change of underwear, find a child's rubbers . . . if they ran back for the family silver or to check the gas burners, they might be wasting their last moment. A minute spent or saved could be the difference between life and death.

Many tried to flee. Families packed into cars and, pressing the accelerator to the floor, tried to outrun it. All the while through the back window, they watched their pursuer gaining on them. Others, thinking they might have to spend the night somewhere without heat, bundled into sweaters and slickers and pulled on boots to slosh through the surging water. They were dressing for certain death, because the burden of heavy clothes would weigh them down in the water.

Timothy Mee owned eight houses on Charlestown Beach and rented seven of them. On Wednesday morning he was working in Woonsocket, a mill town in northern Rhode Island. His wife,

Helen, was alone in the eighth bungalow with their children, Timothy Jr. and six-month-old Jean, and their maid, Agnes Dolan. When the weather turned, Mee left work and drove to Charlestown. The Atlantic was turbulent, magnificent, and terrifying, and if Mee had been on his own, he might have stayed at the beach to watch the storm. But he was a worrier by nature, the kind of man who looked in on his children several times before he went to bed and always double-checked that the gas was off and the doors locked.

Mee was one of the few who believed that the thunder of the sea was a warning as baleful as any the Weather Bureau might issue. By late afternoon, he and Helen had decided to move inland, where the children would be safer, and they offered a ride to their neighbors, the Breckenridges. Four Mees, their maid, three Breckenridges, and two dogs crammed into the car and set out along the shore road through the driving rain. The ocean was slithering across the roadway, but the Mees had only one mile to drive to reach the mainland.

Charlestown Beach is one of the small oceanfront communities along Rhode Island's South County coast. When the sea came ashore, there was no high ground to flee to. Like Westhampton Beach and Napatree, each town had a single road that ran parallel to the ocean. Within moments it was swamped. Across South County and up through Narragansett Bay, a storm surge that one incredulous survivor described as "mountains high" turned these ocean communities into deserts.

Even on the mainland, those who could look across the tidal ponds had no idea what was happening out on the beaches. Visibility was poor and telephones and electricity went out as early as 2:30 P.M. Norman Behneke lived directly across the salt pond from Charlestown Beach. Even when cars were flooding, he said, "it was hard to believe that the dark creeping thing coming up the road was water. Suddenly, as you looked again, it seemed to boil, and out of the haze of the spray there loomed up something which stunned you." Bungalows from Charlestown Beach were riding a racing wave across the pond. Bodies, living and dead, piled up on the shore, battered and entangled by the wreckage of their lives.

A Charlestown Beach survivor described the sight: "Out of nowhere, there came one walloping big wave that seemed to tower above even the highest building, and we were washed for miles, it seemed, before the water subsided and let us down. It took only a few minutes to sweep the beach clean." On the morning of the twenty-first, there were seven hundred houses along this stretch. By nightfall, there was none.

Just down the road at Misquamicut, E. L. Reynolds, assistant fire chief, remembered exhilaration turning to terror: "People on the beach were laughing and joking, trying to put up shutters and fastening windows to keep curtains from getting wet. They thought it was lots of fun. Then suddenly their homes were under twenty or thirty feet of water. Some of the houses just blew up like feathers. I saw one leap seventy-five feet into the air and collapse before it hit the water."

The women of the Mothers Club of Christ Church, Westerly, were having a picnic of carrot and egg salad sandwiches at a Misquamicut beach bungalow. They had postponed their outing twice because of rain, and when the sun shone Wednesday morning, they seized the day. After a Communion service at the church, they went out to Misquamicut for the picnic. Zalee Livingston, a seamstress, brought her four-year-old grandson, but the thundering breakers frightened him. Rector John Tobin, who was returning to the church to conduct a funeral service, took the boy with him. By then, the women were halfway through lunch, their sandwiches more sand than salad. The wind was so strong, they moved their picnic to a sturdier house up the road. In a matter of minutes, swirling seas surrounded it.

In the midst of the storm, a worried husband drove his pickup truck to Christ Church, hoping for news of the women. At dusk, as the winds began subsiding, he and Jack Tobin, the rector's twenty-five-year-old son, rode out to Misquamicut. They drove through the Misquamicut Golf Club to the edge of the fairway. It bordered the saltwater pond, directly across from the picnic spot. "The fairway was covered with chunks of houses," Tobin remembers, "not splinters — big pieces. The man got out of the truck and stumbled over a woman's body. It was his wife. He started giving her artificial respiration." Tobin was studying medicine at Yale, but you didn't have to be a doctor, he said, to know the woman was dead. "Bodies that had washed across the pond from Misquamicut were scattered all over the green." Today, the names of the Mothers of Christ Church are inscribed on a stone monument by the church. It is the only hurricane memorial in the state.

Four hundred died in Rhode Island, 175 along the South County shore. Some oceanfront towns were reduced to mounds of wreckage ten and twelve feet high. Others were wiped away as cleanly as if swept by a broom. There was nothing left except a few telephone poles, a couple of cement steps, a tub or toilet half submerged in the sand.

Timothy Mee drove three-quarters of a mile down the beach road. Another quarter mile and he would reach the mainland. He was driving slowly because the ocean was slapping against the side of the car. The engine flooded. Mee was pumping the gas pedal, holding the key in the ignition, trying to get started again, when a gust picked up the car with everyone in it. Helen and Agnes clutched the children, covering them with their bodies. They were too stunned to scream. What was happening seemed impossible. Their sturdy family car, weighed down by six adults, two children, and two dogs, was tumbling down the road, blowing away like a lost hat or an autumn leaf. Children, adults, and animals were bumping together, banging against the doors one second and the roof the next. The car revolved three times, bounced to a halt, and skidded on its side.

Mee and Breckenridge managed to wrench a door open and pull the women and children from the overturned car. They huddled behind it for protection from the wind. Against such a ferocious force of nature they were as helpless as motes of dust, yet they had to strike out. The water was up to their waists and rising rapidly. They formed a chain, holding hands, when suddenly and without a bit of warning, a terrifying sight appeared from the ocean side. What looked like a polluted lake was bearing down on them. The water was a soiled gray, and towering over it another ten feet was a crest of murky froth — and the whole filthy body of water was rushing toward them. Helen Mee was holding the baby; Agnes Dolan had Timmy. Mee wrapped his arms around them all, hugging them with every ounce of strength he possessed. The lake struck them like a bolt of lightning and tore Mee's family from his grasp.

In Watch Hill, Bob Loomis, a summertime policeman, was off duty and doing some yard work that Wednesday afternoon. He had just finished cutting his lawn when the day took a strange turn: "All of a sudden everything became very, very quiet. Even

the birds seemed to stop singing. The sky began to take on an unusual look. The clouds were very low and moving at an unusual rate of speed." He started to rake up the clippings, but the wind was too quick. It swooped in from the southeast, scattering the piles faster than he could rake.

Loomis lived just up the road from the Watch Hill Lighthouse. About three o'clock, he walked over to check on the forecast. The wind in the Coast Guard tower registered about sixty-five miles per hour, and the barometer was dropping. Small-craft warnings were flying, but the Coast Guard had not received any alert that a hurricane was bearing down on the Northeast.

The first and only warning of a serious storm would come into the Watch Hill station just after Loomis left. By then, water was snaking over the low end of the road. In the few minutes it took him to walk into town, the Great New England Hurricane reached Watch Hill.

About the same time that Officer Loomis left the Coast Guard station, Captain Mahlon Adams was bringing the yacht *Heilu* into the harbor. He was securing it at the Watch Hill Yacht Club with his heaviest hawser when he saw a wave unlike any he had ever seen. It looked "like a roll of cotton." It towered thirty feet, and it was advancing on Fort Road. With a resounding roar, the yacht club split in two and a piano flew out "like a big black bird." The *Heilu* was lifted over the pier and landed in the center of town beside the fire station.

Loomis saw the yacht club go, too: "Lo and behold, it was lifted right up in the air and crashed out into the middle of the bay. As we looked over toward the pavilion, we could see the water coming over the road and rushing into the bay. At the same time, the tide in the bay began to rise so fast we had to jump onto the wall to keep from being submerged." Within minutes "four or five houses came scudding across the bay and we realized that Fort Road was doomed."

Napatree extended west from the yacht club. When the first wave advanced up the beach, it hurdled the old fort, smashed the seawall, and climbed up the front steps of the big-shingled houses. Moments later a second giant wave piled on top of it. Foaming like a mad Cerberus, it broke over the gracious summer houses that lined Fort Road. There were forty-two people in the Napatree cottages when the Atlantic came ashore.

Jane Grey Stevenson and her sister, Mary, lived at Stevecot, the first house on Fort Road, with their maid of many years, Elliefair Price. The Stevenson sisters were as much a part of village life as the Watch Hill merry-go-round. For as long as any-one could remember, they had kept a gift shop in the old school-house. Each morning before opening Miss Stevenson's Little Shop, Jane Grey swam in the ocean. She was a wisp of a woman, with a soft voice and a timid manner, who had always seemed to be in her ebullient sister's shadow. But now that Mary Stevenson had diabetes and did not get into the store much, Jane Grey kept the place going on her own.

On the twenty-first she closed early; she wanted to get back to Mary and Elliefair before the storm got any nastier. About four o'clock, just as the Stevensons were finishing their tea, the first wave broke. It swirled around the cottage and slunk up through the floorboards. Jane Grey packed an overnight bag, and the three women went into the kitchen to wait on the bay side for the Coast Guard boat. They were sure it would pick them up. Mary and Elliefair sat on the kitchen table to keep dry. Jane Grey, knee-deep in water, stood watch at the back door. They assured one another that the boat would be along any moment. They did not feel the slightest bit of fear, because whenever there was high water on Fort Road, the guardsmen always came with a cutter.

From the tower at the Watch Hill station, the Coast Guard saw the first cottages on Fort Road go. It was just a glimpse before the picture dissolved. Sea, sky, and land merged into a single element. Rain and spindrift became so thick, visibility was reduced to about one hundred feet. The barometer was nose-diving, a point every five minutes, and the tower was swaying under winds clocked at 120–150 miles per hour.

The Atlantic pounded the lighthouse point, streaming over it, beating around it — taking out the garden, seawall, road, everything except the glacial rock beneath it. A salty river rushed between the station and the town of Watch Hill, and thirty feet of gray-green water cut a breach between the Coast Guard station and the adjacent lighthouse, making each an island. Officers rigged guidelines from one to the other, but they could not reach their cutters. No rescue boats would be going out to Napatree.

When Bob Loomis reached the center of Watch Hill, a hail of debris was skipping down Bay Street, zipping by the row of smart shops. Picked up by the swirling wind, traffic signs and roof shingles took off like rogue missiles. Ducking and dodging the flying objects, shopkeepers ran from their stores, not even taking time to lock up. A Watch Hill Improvement Society rubbish can whizzed by Loomis's head, nearly taking an ear with it. He was just passing the fire station when the second wave broke: "The water rushed into the firehouse, hit the back wall, and on the rebound washed all three of the fire trucks right out through the closed doors."

In a matter of minutes, the storm was tearing up Watch Hill and washing Napatree into the sea. Loomis figured that if it continued at the same intensity, the loss of life and property would be worse than anything the area had ever experienced. With no car and no means of communicating with the rest of the world, he set out on foot for Westerly, six miles away, to get emergency relief.

Far out on the Napatree beach, the lovebirds Lillian Tetlow and Jack Kinney had gone as far as they could. They had passed the houses and the fort and reached the farthest point when the weather turned. The change was quick and dramatic, as if an awning had been lowered over the day. The sky turned gunmetal gray. The ocean changed to black marble. The sandpipers had vanished — Lillian and Jack did not notice when or where they went. Suddenly afraid, the sweethearts started back. On the beach, the wind now in their faces, the waves breaking higher and higher on the sand, it could have been a different day. The perfect beach morning was gone without a trace. Even the colors seemed to wash away.

When they turned toward Watch Hill, they felt as if they had stepped into a grainy black-and-white movie. They began to run, but the gusting wind pushed them back. They bent into it, pressed against it. Lillian clung to Jack's arm, and he pulled her along. Rain like nails pounded them. Foam flew, and rain, and spindrift. They could not see where sea and sky met, or hear each other over the wind. It whined as it worked, whipping sand, spray, and rain into a murky batter, adding broken shells and splintered driftwood, and hurling it in their faces. They sank into the sand, each step harder than the one before. Lillian began crying, and they were both shaking with cold and wet and fear.

They made it back as far as the old fort and staggered in, too tired to try to reach their car or one of the houses, wanting only to get out of the storm. The two clammers had burrowed in, too, and the four of them huddled in a bunker room, winded, stunned, hypnotized by the voice of the storm. It had switched keys to a haunting keen that got into the brain.

To longtime Napatree residents, it seemed as if the impossible was happening. The Atlantic Ocean was beating the houses on Fort Road to pieces. There was no escape. Road, cars, and every means of communication were gone, washed away in the first waves.

Jeff and Catherine Moore had no phone, no electricity, no water, and ten people in the house: their four children; May Doherty, who had been Catherine's maid of honor and was Aunt May to the Moore children; and three in help: Andy Pupillo; their cook, Loretta; and sixteen-year-old Nancy, who helped out with the younger girls. While Jeff got up from his sickbed to board up the first-floor windows, Catherine began preparing the house for a long, dark night. She collected all the candles and matches she could find and put some on each floor. Then she went hunting for life jackets. She could find only three. She gave one to Aunt May and strapped the youngest girls, Cathy and Margaret, into the others.

To the four Moore children, the storm was the most exciting thing that had happened all summer, and they were loving every minute of it. They ran from window to window, whooping at each huge breaker that crashed against the seawall, sending spume flying. Jeff and Catherine were trying to secure their home without letting the children know how worried they were. The storm was furious, walloping the houses on either side of theirs. They didn't want the children to see the Fort Road houses collapsing, and they wanted to keep their family together in one place, quiet and accounted for. The safest spot they could think of was the garage, with its thick cement walls. Catherine bundled the girls, their seven cats and kittens, and Aunt May into the Buick, turned on the car radio, and supplied plenty of snacks and drinks to keep them occupied. Geoffrey and Major, his Newfoundland, got in the Ford beach wagon.

In the Burke cottage, a couple of houses down from the Moores', Jerry Shea, Ed Fiddes, and Joe Reardon were making renovations. The three carpenters didn't realize how serious the storm was until they were packing up to leave for the day. Joe Reardon glanced out a back window and started yelling: *Where do you think you're going? Come back!* Their car had taken off with all their tools, and no driver.

The carpenters made a dash for the old fort, thinking a concrete bunker would be a secure spot to wait out the storm. They went a couple of yards when the wind tackled them. Jerry Shea felt as if he had been hit by the Seven Blocks of Granite, Fordham's then impregnable defensive line. The men retreated to the house. By then, the first floor was flooded and more water was flowing in fast. They headed for the stairs with the ocean a step behind them. As they reached the second floor, a wave took out the stairway. Holed up in one of the bedrooms, they stretched out on the beds. Jerry Shea linked his hands behind his head. "Ain't this the life, boys! We may as well wait for the end in comfort."

The words were no sooner spoken than the beds skidded across the room and careened into the opposite wall. The room jolted like a train car derailing and tilted at a 45° angle. A second tremendous wave had taken out the center of the house.

The carpenters jumped out of bed and raced for the attic. They found the door leading up to it closed. They jiggled the knob, banged on the door, pushed against it with the force of their combined weight — all to no avail. The attic door was wedged tight. Attacking it with chairs, the desperate men smashed a hole and crawled through. In the attic they forced open the dormer windows, and when the water rushed in, they climbed onto the roof.

It was icy cold. Jerry Shea thought he saw the Moores' house floating by. The house in motion was actually the one they were riding. A few moments later the roof split, ending their ride abruptly. Jerry and Ed were flung into the water. Joe held on. He could not swim a stroke. The water was full of wreckage twisting and crashing in the current. As Jerry Shea began to surface, he was crowned — anything could have hit him, a car, a kitchen stool, the deck of a boat. He went down again. He was alone when he resurfaced. He couldn't find Ed or Joe. Shea rode with the current until a mattress came by: "No sooner had I pulled myself onto it than a gust of wind and water took me, the mattress and all, and I was flung for some distance, landing on the floating roof of a cottage." There was a cable on it that looked like a lightning rod wire. He wound his arm around it, thinking at least his body would be found and his wife and four children could collect his life insurance.

In the cottage next door to the Moores', Jim Nestor was begging his aunt to hurry, but Ann Nestor would not be rushed. There were six Nestor sisters, all unmarried except one, and two brothers. The sisters wintered in Westerly and summered together on Napatree. Jim, the youngest of the nephews and nieces, had been spending summers with his aunts ever since he was old enough to be on his own. He would be starting his sophomore year at Brown at the end of the week.

On this stormy afternoon Jim was alone in the cottage with his aunt Ann, and the Nestors' two maids. Although it was a substantial house with a huge fireplace in the living room and eight bedrooms, by 4:30 P.M. the Nestors had decided to evacuate. Ann Nestor, who taught English at Westerly High School, would not think of leaving home without an overnight bag. "Don't hurry me, Jim," she said as she packed. "All in good time."

With her customary aplomb and in her own good time, Ann Nestor, overnight case in hand, led the way out the back door, trailed by her two maids — Margaret Tetlow, a widow with four young children, and Ethel Watson. The three women were dressed for the storm in raincoats, hats, and boots. Ann Nestor and Margaret Tetlow stepped out first, just as the sea broke over the cottage. It swept them away instantly. Seeing them go, Ethel Watson panicked and jumped into the swirling water after them. Jim was the last to leave the house. The three women had vanished.

The Nestors' house had a wide porch on the side that faced the Moores'. The space between the two houses, usually a patch of sand, had become a raging river. Wrapping himself around a porch post, Jim held on. Wind and water hammered at him, ripped off his clothes, then beat down the house around him. Jim jumped off the porch as it collapsed and plunged into the wild river.

When the rain spoiled their game at the Watch Hill Golf Club, the three friends — Harriet Moore, who was married to Jeff's brother Cy, Violet Cottrell, and Denise O'Brien — trooped back to Harriet's Napatree house to see the waves. The turbulent ocean was magnificent. The women were standing at the window admiring it when the glass in the porch blew out, taking the porch furniture with it. The next thing they knew, Harriet's metal glider-couch was flying across the front yard and careening through the dining room window of the next-door cottage, a distance of maybe fifty yards, and waves were breaking on the front porch. The time was about four o'clock.

With the Atlantic Ocean at her doorstep, Harriet's first thought was her new living room curtains. The water would ruin them. The friends went to work. They pushed the piano in front of the porch doors to keep them from blowing open, then they took down the curtains, folded them carefully, and put them away in a chest of drawers. They had no sooner finished the task than the house next door, with Harriet's glider still in the dining room, sailed off its foundation into the bay.

Unbeknownst to the watching women, Herb Greenman, the caretaker, and his friend Frank Pasetti were inside the disappearing house. They had been nailing up the winter shutters when the roof collapsed. Greenman was pinned under it, his ribs broken. He called to Frank. There was no answer. Greenman was sure that he was going to die beneath the roof. All at once, the house began to tremble. It felt like an earthquake. Room by room shattered. Suddenly freed, Greenman found himself being tossed in the turmoil of Little Narragansett Bay. It seemed as if he had exchanged one death sentence for another. Piercing pain from his broken ribs made every movement agony. He did not have the strength to save himself. Greenman had given up hope when a bathtub bumped by him carrying a rag doll. The doll seemed to be riding the wind gusts. Though tattered and torn, she was still bobbing along. Alone in the mad sea, Herb Greenman laughed out loud. Pain seared through his chest, but he didn't care. "Old girl," he shouted over the tumult, "if you can make it, so can I."

While Harriet Moore and her friends were watching the house next door disappear, the ocean moved into her living room. It brushed the piano aside like a piece of sheet music and swamped the first floor. Harriet wasn't afraid, though. Life was fine and her house was strong. A little water, even a few feet of the Atlantic Ocean running through the first floor, was a nuisance to clean up, not a danger.

Harriet Chappell Moore was a society girl from New London, a young woman to the manner born who would have gone hungry if she didn't have a cook. She was a marvelous hostess, an avid golfer, a wonderful gardener, and, at age thirty-two, a new mother. After years of trying to have children of their own, she and her husband, Cy, had recently adopted Mary, a six-year-old with strawberry blond pigtails, very blue eyes, and a captivating smile. With no lights, no electricity, a house full of water, and little Mary to think about, the three friends decided the most sensible course of action would be to drive back to Watch Hill, which was higher ground. Harriet's cottage was one of the closest to town, so it would take only a few minutes.

Violet and Denise went out to the concrete garage behind the house while Harriet went upstairs to get Mary and their maid, Margaret Kane. She found them surrounded by mops and towels, trying unsuccessfully to keep the ocean out of the bedrooms. From the upstairs rooms it felt as if the house were under a cataract. Tons of water were spilling over it. Harriet could see the spume on the underside of the waves through her bedroom window. Even then she didn't think they were in danger. She sent Mary and Margaret down to the garage while she gathered up a few necessities — a dry coat for Cy, a raincoat and rubbers for Mary. On the way downstairs, she stopped to put five letters, which she had written that morning, in a high place, safely above the rising water.

Harriet believed her house could weather any storm, but Violet and Denise had no such illusions. All the Fort Road houses were solidly built, and they were splintering. When Harriet came down, they told her they were stranded. Even if they could get their cars out, there was no hope of driving away. Fort Road was under ten feet of water, and the garage was filling fast. The friends were trying to devise a survival plan when an earsplitting roar shook the ground they stood on. The house and garage began to break up around them. Harriet scooped up Mary, and the four women made a dash for the house. They bolted up the back stairs to the kitchen door. The door was locked.

The back stairs were a short flight of perhaps six steps enclosed by a latticework wall. Harriet, Mary, and Margaret crowded together on the top step. Violet and Denise stood below them, gripping the rail. With each wave, the stairs groaned and shook. They felt the treads moving under their feet, and through the lattice they could see gray surf thundering by. They masked their fear with humor. Denise was wondering aloud if the living room curtains were faring better than they were, when a third wave came. With a frightening grinding sound, all the stairs caved in except the top one where Harriet, Mary, and Margaret stood. The last Harriet saw of her friends was the soles of their shoes as the ocean swept them away.

Sucked into the vortex, Violet and Denise struggled to keep their heads above the warring water. Swimming was impossible, but they tried to stay together and buoy each other through the terror. "A very friendly mattress appeared and we climbed aboard," Denise recalled. "During our sail across the bay, the mattress became soggy, so we hailed a roof and changed horses midstream." The two friends hugged the roof. Although they were inches apart, they were screaming at the top of their lungs to hear each other above the storm:

"Shouldn't we go back for Harriet?"

"I don't think we can, Vi."

"We can't leave her there."

Violet barely spoke the words when there was a cracking noise that she described as "the most horrifying I have ever heard." Harriet's house split squarely down the middle and erupted like a volcano. Beds, bureaus, chairs, mattresses, everything shot into the air like clowns out of a circus cannon. The friends knew there wasn't a chance that anyone had survived.

"God forgive us," Violet said.

CHAPTER 16

Providence

Half a dozen radios were playing in the appliance department of the Outlet Company, the biggest department store
in downtown Providence. *Backstage Wife* was humming from the
Philco console: *"Can a small-town girl from Iowa find happiness with
one of America's most handsome actors, Larry Noble, matinee idol of
a million other women . . . ?"* Anthony Eden was speaking over a
sleek Emerson table model, denouncing Chamberlain's "straw
peace": *"We slither ever closer to the abyss. The idea that safety can be
purchased by throwing a small state to the wolves is a fatal delusion."*

It was all background noise to Jimmy Brennan. Jimmy managed the Outlet's radio department, and he had learned to program his attention like one of the machines he sold, tuning the
broadcasts in or out at will. He usually listened for the afternoon
weather. When he heard a bulletin about a hurricane in Connecticut, he went downstairs to tell his friend Florence Simmons
in the ladies' shoe department.

Florence laughed at him. "Oh, Jimmy, there'll never be a
hurricane. We've never had a hurricane." She was still smiling a

few minutes later when a woman ran into the store, incoherent and crying hysterically — something about her baby blowing out of her arms. Florence could not make any sense of the story. It sounded crazy — as crazy as a hurricane in New England. From inside the Outlet, she couldn't hear the wind or see what the weather was doing. Florence was trying to calm the woman when a policeman came in, his cap gone and his shoes squeaking with water. He was carrying a boy about two years old in his arms.

The Hurricane of 1938 had reached the capital of Rhode Island. Trees were falling and pedestrians were having trouble keeping their footing. In a matter of minutes, water was washing over the running boards of the cars in front of the Outlet and filling the store's cellar. Refrigerators and stoves floated up from the basement.

A few blocks away in the newsroom of the *Providence Journal*, the editors were laying out a sports extra when a warning clattered over the Teletype machine: *Serious storm headed for southern New England. Tropical disturbance will cross LI Sound and reach the Conn-RI border early tonight.* The time was about 3:40 P.M. The *Journal* editors were debating whether to insert a weather story in the sports extra when the presses stopped, ending the discussion. The city turned black, as if a municipal plug had been pulled. In the murky light, everything not cemented down was flying or floating. Hundreds of plate-glass store windows popped and their contents spilled into the street. Streetlights shattered, raining splinters of glass that jabbed like daggers on the wind, bloodying many trying to flee the storm.

A rave review in the morning *New York Herald Tribune* had described *Old Haven* (Houghton Mifflin, $2.50), a new novel by David Cornel de Jong, as "a well-wrought story set in a landscape borrowed from Breughel." The author wasn't reading his glowing notice, though. He was marooned in the Providence Arcade. The first indoor shopping mall, the Arcade runs the width of a city block and opens on two busy downtown streets, Weybosset and Westminster. It was designed in 1825 in the style of a Greek Revival temple with six massive granite pillars at either entrance. Three floors of shops connected by long, open iron balconies overlook the ground-floor atrium, and above the atrium is a long glass skylight.

When the hurricane roared in, the Arcade became a wind tunnel. Shoppers clutching their bags, salesgirls tottering on spike heels, and bootblacks, their polishing boxes slung over their shoulders, tried to dash across Weybosset Street. The wind stopped them. It was "an invisible wall in front of us, holding us impotently suspended," de Jong remembered. A store window crashed inches away. A shard of glass slashed the throat of a woman just ahead of him. Her blood splattered his face. When he reached her, the wind pushed them into a revolving door with the crowd of shoppers, two and three in a single compartment, and spun them repeatedly. De Jong took refuge in the third-floor office of a lawyer friend. From there he watched as the hurricane drove up Narragansett Bay.

The wind came first, brining sporadic showers, spraying spindrift miles inland, filling the air with brine. If you licked your lips in Providence, thirty miles from the nearest beach, you tasted salt. The ocean was a step behind. The narrow head of the bay compressed the storm surge into an ever higher dome of water. Spilling into the downtown district, the rushing water tore down wharves and hurled a couple of coal barges across Water Street. It swept into the heart of the city, swishing through the streets, bolting around corners, gurgling into stores and offices, and surrounding City Hall.

Solomon Brandt, a printer, was working in his shop on the second floor of a city office building. "The first time I looked out, I recall distinctly there was no unusual amount of water," he recounted. "As I returned again from the presses no more than five minutes from the previous time, I saw the most unusual sight I had ever seen in all my life. The water was rushing through the streets. It rose almost as fast as if you held a glass in front of a spigot."

The bay washed over Providence — six feet, ten, twelve — over the roofs of cars, over the tops of trolleys — fifteen, seventeen feet — inundating three miles of industrial waterfront and the mile-square business district. In thirty minutes the service station where Lally Dwyer stopped for gas in the morning on the way to her job at the telephone company, the newsstand where she bought the morning *Journal*, the soda fountain counter where she ate lunch, were submerged.

Workers trying to leave their offices at five o'clock plunged into a whitecapped lake, 17.6 feet at its deepest point. Pedestrians wrapped themselves around lampposts and clung to fire escapes. Drivers who managed to get free of their cars swam into stores. Trapped passengers dove through the windows of trolley cars. In the gray, engulfing water, cars and trolleys disappeared, their batteries shorted, and a muffled din echoed from the submerged vehicles. Car horns blared and trolley bells clanged like the bells of hell, and their lights glowed eerily through the water.

Almost fifteen hundred moviegoers, marooned in the city's five downtown theaters, crowded into the highest balcony seats as the water rushed in. At the RKO Albee, the manager swam over the orchestra seats to reach the balcony stairs. Pierce's shoe store on the corner of Dorrance Street, where the walls were stacked floor to ceiling with shoe boxes, filled with water so fast that the

clerk and a customer were sent scooting up to the top of the sliding ladder. They hung there watching black-and-white saddle
shoes, cordovan wing tips, and patent leather high-heeled pumps
with open toes and ankle straps step out on their own. Down the
street, the H. L. Wood Boat Co. launched rowboats through the
windows to rescue the stranded.

From the third-floor office de Jong watched the city flood and
later wrote a vivid account for *Yankee* magazine:

> A gray light seemed pressed between the high buildings
> and weighed on murky, churning water in the street.
> People floundered in all directions, at once abetted or op-
> posed every inch of the way by the awful winds. Directly
> below us, an old man, neck deep in water, lifted his hands
> and sank. We craned our necks but never saw him again.
> He was drowned. "Must have been drunk, the crazy fool,"
> three men said simultaneously. But their eyes said he could
> not have been drowned, not there, our eyes are crazy. The
> men turned away from the window, all three, and lighted
> cigarettes.

As de Jong continued watching the bizarre floating parade
below, a blond mannequin from a dress shop swam into the
street: "Holding her head high, her visage vacant, never sinking,
she pirouetted on the flood like a well-mannered debutante."
Next came a desk with a pencil sharpener clamped on one corner,
its arm revolving in the wind; red balls went flying by "like puffed
exotic fish"; then a chain of people chin-deep in water. The last
link was a woman. Her grasp slipped, and the rushing tide pulled
the others away. They struggled back and linked arms with her
again. She slipped loose a second and a third time, too frightened

and hysterical to hold fast, and each time the others battled the current and went back for her.

De Jong was riveted on the human drama until someone in the office shouted, "Look at the blonde!" The mannequin "had tilted her head through a store window. She seemed to be peering haughtily inside" when a heavy beam borne on the rushing water smashed into her, and crushed her. A woman in the office screamed. Then the tension broke, and everyone laughed.

Seven people perished in the streets of downtown Providence, three men and four women, drowned or crushed in their cars. Roaring white water swept one man to his death right in front of the steps of City Hall, as incredulous workers watched from the windows. A couple of blocks away, Leo Carter, the janitor at the *Providence Tribune* building, lowered ropes from the fire escape and, one by one, pulled five people out of the water to safety.

At Union Station, where passengers waited for trains that never came, the wind took off the metal roof and rolled it up like a rug. The station was beyond the reach of the floodwater, and many found refuge there. One man, Joseph Vogel, was dressed to the nines in morning coat and top hat. Vogel was on his way to his wedding at the Narragansett Hotel in the heart of downtown Providence. He nipped into the station to get out of the storm and became marooned there. While his bride and her family waited at the Narragansett, strangers seeking refuge from the storm poured into the reception room, ate all the food, and drank all the champagne. The Vogels were finally married in the evening by candlelight. They waded a few blocks across town to the Biltmore Hotel. Although the first floor was submerged, they were offered a candle along with the wedding suite.

In Rhode Island's major banks, floodwater inundated the vaults and seeped through the seams of safe-deposit boxes. The next morning, bank managers strung clotheslines the length of the vaults, and moneyed Rhode Islanders trekked down College Hill, poured the foul water out of their boxes, and hung their stock certificates on the line to dry. One loss was irretrievable. The original charter of Brown University, written in 1765 by hand on parchment paper, had been stored in a downtown bank for safekeeping. The salt in the floodwater stiffened the parchment and erased the ink.

All through Narragansett Bay, the hurricane emptied marinas and demolished country clubs, yacht clubs, casinos, and beach pavilions. At Rocky Point, an amusement park on the bay where Rutherford B. Hayes made the first telephone call ever dialed by an American president, the famous roller coaster collapsed. The cavernous restaurant (with seating for a thousand) was reduced to the boilers, and the water rose so high that bathing suits dangled from the beechwood trees still standing after the storm.

At Narragansett Pier, across the bay from Jamestown, thirty-foot waves crushed breakwater boulders and gouged out Ocean Road, which meanders south to Point Judith. They pushed Sherry's Pavilion, operated by the fashionable New York restaurateur Louis Sherry, across the road, beat down Palmer's Bathhouse just to the south, and left the pricey Dunes Club, a mile or so north, in ruins. All that was left of the Narragansett Pier Casino was the massive Norman tower designed by Stanford White.

In Newport, where the Vanderbilts and Astors entertained in high style and summer getaways were modeled after Versailles, trees cracked, a wing tore away, a roof caved in. Otherwise, the grand mansions were unharmed. Most of them occupied high ground, where only the wind could reach them. In the lower-lying areas of Newport, the damage was much worse. The *Promised Land,* a 135-foot fishing boat, spun across the harbor and was tossed up on the city wharf. Out on Ocean Drive, wash-outs were a hazard, and Bailey's Beach and the Clambake Club, favorite hangouts of the wealthy and privileged, were demolished. At the more egalitarian Easton Beach, the storm reduced the carnival-style carousel and roller coaster to kindling wood. Many were happy to see them go.

Hartley Ward of Newport kept a record of the hurricane day. "The whole summer season had been one of most unusual weather," he wrote, "nothing like it had been noted in Newport in many years." At two o'clock Wednesday afternoon, the sun was still shining on Narragansett Bay, but the surf was brushing over the seawalls and the tide was running high. By 3:30 P.M., the skies were threatening; by four o'clock, the gale had reached Newport. As Hartley Ward reported:

> There was no holding things down and it was all one's life was worth to walk in the streets. The tide was way up in Thames Street. The wind was coming in terrible gusts, pulling trees up by the roots, and knocking people down. Ambulances were rushing, sirens screeching through the din, signs clanging along the sidewalks, the horns of five hundred submerged automobiles blowing and the rain pelting down in torrents. The steeple of the First Baptist Church tottered and tumbled into the street, its bell clanging a terrible dirge as it landed.

Other parts of the island took a thrashing, too. One of the worst hit was Island Park, Portsmouth, a finger of beachland at the northeastern end. The next day some Island Park residents found their homes in a peach orchard a mile away, and they were the lucky ones. Nineteen died in Island Park.

The colonial village of Bristol, home of the first Fourth of July parade, was pummeled and cut off from the rest of the state for two days. The hurricane smashed the Bristol Lobster Pot, one of the most popular seafood restaurants in Rhode Island, and wrecked the Herreshoff boatyards, where Captain Nathaniel Herreshoff, known as "the Wizard of Bristol," had designed and built eight consecutive America's Cup defenders. After 1938 new technologies and demands for sleeker, swifter styles would relegate the classic sloops to history.

CHAPTER 17

The Tempest

In towns and villages across Rhode Island, schools were letting out as the hurricane stormed in. Children, dismissed into the fury, were greeted by wind and rain, crashing trees, and crackling live wires.

In Jamestown the wind was kicking up as Norm Caswell began his afternoon bus run. The Caswells had lived on the island long enough to know every cove on the coast and every quirk in the weather. Norm and his brothers fished the bay waters every season. They had ridden out squalls, northeasters, and line storms in their thirty-foot skiff. Before the twenty-first, Norm would have told you that nobody knew September gales better than he did.

Caswell usually made two trips on his afternoon run. He took the kids who lived on the north end home first, then looped back to pick up the Beavertail group. This afternoon, though, with a squall coming, the teachers were anxious to close up school and get everyone home. Norm piled all the kids onto the bus and started off for the north end, confident that he could beat the storm.

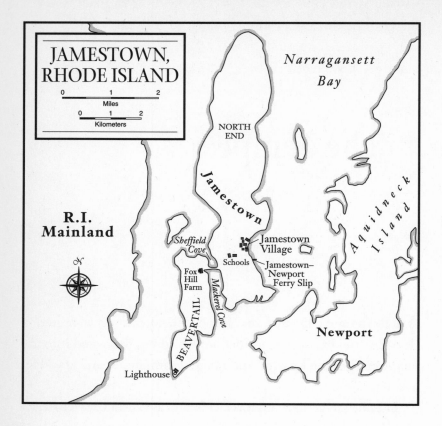

At the U.S. War College in Newport, Captain C. W. Magruder was not so sure. The navy brass had been taking its cue from the D.C. Weather Bureau. "Everyone expected the storm to pass well clear of Nantucket and we would have our usual rather heavy but not serious northeaster," Magruder said. By three o'clock, he was questioning the forecast. An east-southeast gale and torrential rain were pummeling the islands. Houses on the east shore of Mackerel Cove were drenched in spray.

By four o'clock, cars and boats were bobbing in the harbor like apples in a tub. The chain of stores built on pilings by the wharf broke up. Bunny Ellis's barroom and Old Man Sheehan's tailor shop were torn to pieces. The coal trestle ended up at the

Bayside Inn, a quarter mile away, and the White Nook restaurant, a favorite with ferry riders, crossed Conanicut Avenue and settled down on Mrs. Bowen's front porch.

The ferry slip was going, too. The ferryboat captains decided to make a run for the comparative safety of Newport, where the harbor was deeper. *Beavertail*, the last of the old paddle wheelers, left first with only captain and crew aboard. She was halfway across the channel when the hurricane caught her. It pushed her four or five miles north up the bay, and discarded her on a jagged rock, her wooden hull pierced, her engines and boiler ruined. All hands scrambled to safety.

A few minutes later, "with three blasts of her horn, black smoke pouring out of her stack and under a full head of steam, Jamestown's pride, the *Governor Carr*, moved out of her ferry slip and disappeared in the blinding rain." The passengers and cars that had boarded for the three o'clock trip were still aboard. A couple of hundred yards out, a hawser tangled in the propeller and the *Governor Carr* lost power. The big boat drifted in the high seas until wind and wave drove her back toward Jamestown. Lifted on the surging tide, she leapfrogged rocks and seawalls and came to rest on Webster Weatherill's lawn, up the bay and across the road from the dock. The beached ferry was listing at a 45° angle but otherwise unharmed.

Joe Matoes left the Jamestown school yard alone and turned his milk truck down North Road. Rain like sheet metal slanted off the bay, reducing visibility to zero. Matoes scrunched over the steering wheel, peering through the clear half circle the windshield wipers made. He had a fireplug build — short, square, and powerful — yet he had to grip the steering wheel with both hands to hold the truck on the road. Branches were cracking. Outdoor furniture, weather vanes, bicycles — everything that wasn't nailed down — was winging across the island, turning the road into an obstacle course. The wind sharpened. It stripped the leaves from the trees, slashed them into bits and pieces, and splattered them against the houses, painting white clapboards green.

Matoes's truck was shaking and swerving. He crawled down North Road, every yard gained with difficulty, and turned right onto the causeway. Beavertail and his farm lay at the end. Mackerel Cove was on his left, Sheffield Cove on his right, and between them only the narrow milelong sandbar, one hundred yards at its widest point, nothing more than a sandy path through the sea with a strip of macadam poured down the middle. The bay was breaking across it. Three or four other cars were scattered along the road. They were empty, their drivers nowhere in sight.

Matoes's truck flooded in the rising water. He abandoned it and struggled along the road. Billy Ordiner and his mother passed him on their way back from seeing the surf at Beavertail. Their car stalled somewhere along the causeway. The wind screeched through Mackerel Cove, obliterating every other sound. It lifted the roof off the beach pavilion in one piece and sent it sailing. Like an enormous hat, the roof flew across the road, up over Sheffield Cove, and out of sight. The next morning, it was found whole and unharmed in a pasture on the Watson Farm, a couple of miles due north. No one will ever know for sure whether the same gust that lifted the roof off the pavilion also picked up the Ordiners' car with Billy and his mother inside.

Joe Matoes's clothes were soaked, his face blistered from the biting wind. He couldn't hear the slosh of the water as he splashed through. When he finally reached the edge of his fields, Fox Hill Farm was in darkness, as if locked up for the night. He looked back. Through the mire, he could just discern the bulk of the school bus crossing the causeway. There were eight children still on board. Four of them were his. He waved his arms frantically, trying to signal Norm Caswell to turn back.

At Napatree all the Fort Road houses were gone, except Jeff and Catherine Moore's. Most of the homes were those wonderful weathered-shingle New England summer houses. But the Moores' place was a huge barn of a house, three stories high, painted yellow with brown trim and built like a fortress to withstand any weather. It was anchored in cement and to further protect it, on the ocean side, there was a thick, deep seawall.

At first Jeff and Catherine thought they could hold back the hurricane by barricading their home with extra doors and shutters. But the wind taunted and trumpeted, hurling tons of water against the house. Doctor's orders forgotten, Jeff pressed against the front door, trying to hold back the Atlantic Ocean single-handedly. The living room window shattered. The dining room windows caved in next, casements and all. By 4:30 P.M., all the downstairs doors and windows were gone. The Moores' only chance was to let the ocean run through the first floor and wait out the storm upstairs. If the water didn't undermine the foundation, they would be safe.

Catherine got the girls and Aunt May out of the Buick and rapped on the window of the other car: "Geoffrey, come out. We're all going upstairs."

The boy sat in the backseat with his arm around Major and did not budge. "Why?" he yelled over the static blare of the car radio and the baying wind.

"Because the house is going to collapse," his mother shouted back. She thought that would scare him into the house.

Carrying Margaret, she led the children back inside, splashing through knee-deep water to the staircase. The entire household gathered upstairs in a second-floor bedroom — Jeff and Catherine, their three daughters, Aunt May, Andy, Nancy, who couldn't swim, and Loretta, who kept crying, "Oh, Mrs. Moore, my baby! I have to get my baby." Catherine went to work getting everyone organized. She was piling sweaters and coats on the bed so everyone would be warm through the cold, heatless night when she realized that her son was missing. Andy Pupillo ran back downstairs through the mounting water. He found Geoffrey still sitting in the station wagon, trying to soothe his frightened dog. Major would not leave the car, and Geoffrey would not leave Major.

Persuasion requires time, and it took a considerable amount of persuasion to convince the boy that Major would be safe in the car. The dog was a powerful swimmer, strong enough to pull a dory. By the time Geoffrey agreed to go into the house, the water was waist-deep. It was flowing in the front door, through the first floor, and cascading down the back steps like a waterfall. He and Andy had to fight their way inside. They crawled through a hole in the kitchen door, slunk along the back hallway, and climbed over a snarl of tables and chairs at the foot of the stairway. Finally, they reached the temporary safety of the second floor.

At the other end of Napatree, three shared a single narrow back step. Harriet Moore was hugging her daughter, Mary, in her arms, the child white with fear, too frightened for tears. Their maid, Margaret Kane, just a girl herself and certain she would never see her own mother again, was praying to God, to the Blessed Mother, to every saint she could remember, for a miracle.

A tremendous uproar drowned out her prayers, and a third wave swept in, flinging volumes of water over them.

"Gracious, there goes the kitchen stove," Margaret cried.

"Yes, and the icebox, too," Harriet sputtered.

A fourth wave followed fast on the third. The house surrendered, and the three were cast into the bay like a single, tangled creature — Mary wrapped around her mother's neck, Harriet and Margaret clutching each other. Eyes and ears, mouths and nostrils filled with salt water. Margaret grabbed a piece of roofing floating by, and they wriggled onto it. The makeshift raft was good-sized, about as big as a bed, but they had trouble staying on. Shingles were sliding off, causing them to slide, too.

The younger Moore children were weeping. Through the bedroom window they had watched the house next door blow down. They saw Ann Nestor step outside, wrapped against the weather in a scarf and hat. A huge wave came, and suddenly she wasn't there. All at once, the storm was not fun. It was frightening.

Eight-year-old Cathy was crying to her mother, "We're all going to die. I don't want to die, and I don't want you to die."

"You won't die" — her mother tried to calm her — "but you might have to swim."

Margaret began to sob. "I don't want to swim."

In the midst of the wailing, Aunt May got down on her knees beside the bed and began reciting the rosary aloud. Refusing to be drowned out by a nasty storm, she prayed at the top of her lungs. *Hail Mary, full of grace. The Lord is with thee.* Catherine tried to join in but was distracted. Undeterred, Aunt May continued. She was on the second Sorrowful Mystery when a wild-eyed boy burst into the bedlam. He was tall and lanky with thick curly black hair that was plastered over his skull like a bathing cap. Jim Nestor, naked except for his B.V.D.s, collapsed on the bed and sank into the mound of clothes Catherine had collected. He had been fighting off a bad cold all week. Now he was breathless, heaving, and barely coherent. Jeff asked him where the others were.

Jim gasped, "Gone. They're all gone. What are we going to do?"

"There's not much we can do. The most important thing is to stay together. No matter what, stay together."

Until then, Catherine Moore had been focusing on the details — Geoffrey was wearing only faded corduroys. He should put on a shirt . . . Cathy needed to take off her sandals . . . Margaret should drink some milk. As she looked at Jim, the full horror of their situation gripped her, and she began to lose hope. The next few minutes would determine their fate. They all took off their shoes, and the girls took off their dresses in case they had to swim. The room was rocking like a dock. They waited, praying constantly — sometimes silently, sometimes aloud.

The house took a sudden swing and began to collapse beneath them. They raced down the hall and up the stairs to the third-floor attic. Behind them, the second floor dropped like an elevator. Catherine looked back. At the bottom of the stairs where her daughters' room had been, the Atlantic Ocean roared. As she watched, her pink curtains washed out of the linen closet into the sea. Then the water started up the third-floor stairs.

The Moores' attic had a maid's room and a bathroom. There were windows at either end, which might break at any time, a floor that could easily give way, and a V-shaped roof. Jeff punched out the bathroom window so they would have an escape hatch, cutting his hand in the process. There was blood everywhere. A torrent of water poured through the jagged hole.

Ten-year-old Anne volunteered to swim for help: "If you get a rope, you can tie it around my waist. Shall I go, Daddy?"

"Don't go, Anne," her father said.

Just then most of the roof blew off, taking with it three walls of the maid's room. All that remained was the floor, which made a perfect raft. A pair of iron pipes stuck up through the flooring. Catherine caught hold of one pipe and sat down with Cathy on her lap. Jeff sat down and wrapped his leg around the other pipe. He had Margaret in his arms. Aunt May sat between Catherine and Jeff, holding his arm in a grip of iron. Anne wrapped her arms around her father from the back. Geoffrey sat in front of his mother with Andy. Jim held on to Loretta and Nancy. With the remaining portion of roof serving as a sail of sorts, they were launched into the hurricane sea.

At 6:15 P.M., Bob Loomis staggered into the Westerly police station. He had stumbled through the storm for more than two hours. Loomis, always a snappy dresser, was as handsome as a matinee idol, and he cut quite a figure in his motorcycle police uniform and shaded goggles. Now, though, his face was raw from the lash of the wind and the sting of the salt and sand it carried. His sodden clothes were as heavy as a suit of mail and plastered to his body. Shaking from exhaustion and from the horror he had witnessed, Loomis blurted out the freakish story. Westerly, located on the banks of the Pawcatuck River, was experiencing hurricane winds and flooding, but nothing as terrible as the storm surge that engulfed Napatree, and Loomis had to convince the incredulous police chief that his story was neither a crazy fantasy nor a reckless exaggeration. It was the simple truth. Fort Road had ceased to be.

Mackerel Cove is the gentlest spot on Jamestown, a deep half circle between the main island and Beavertail. Generations of children have learned to swim in its gentle waters. Even in stormy weather, the cove doesn't menace. No rough surf. No undertow. No riptide. Just the occasional jellyfish, translucent and slippery, and the seagulls, foam white and slate gray, fat, cocky, and bold as brass. If swimmers leave their lunch unattended, the seagulls will march right over and help themselves.

On this Wednesday, though, even Mackerel Cove was treacherous. By the time the school bus reached the causeway, beach cabanas were floating in the bay and waves were breaking over the road. Once Norm Caswell started across, there was no turning back. The water was up to the hubcaps of the bus. Caswell plowed through. Midway across the causeway, the bus stalled. He tried to get it started again, but the engine would not turn over. Caswell went out into the gale. The wind was probably a hundred miles an hour, and the bus was rocking like a dinghy caught in a tanker's wake. Breakers were crashing against it. Caswell edged along behind the bus, pressed against it, head down, body hunched, trying to protect himself from the volleys of wind and the shingles that were shooting across the road from the beach pavilion. By the time he reached the back door of the bus he was winded. He rested against it to catch his breath, then pried it open. Caswell was afraid the children would be trapped inside. Leaning against the door to keep it from slamming shut, he began to help them out.

Clayton Chellis had his little sister, Marion, by the hand when they stepped off the bus into the waters of Narragansett Bay. Clayton believed he could swim in anything. He was eleven years old and fearless, but he had never experienced anything like a hurricane. Joseph Matoes was holding his youngest sister, Eunice, by the hand and nudging his other sisters ahead of him toward the door. Dorothy and Theresa were rigid with fear and inching forward with small, stiff steps like mechanical dolls. If the school bus had stalled on any other day, they could have walked home. Their farm was at the end of the causeway, less than a quarter of a mile away. Joseph coaxed them forward: *We're almost home. Don't be scared, I'm right behind you.*

Over the howl of the hurricane, Norm cupped his mouth and shouted to the children to form a line, holding hands. Clayton was at one end with Marion, next came the Matoeses — Dorothy, Theresa, Joseph, and Eunice. John and Constantine Gianitis hung back in the bus, pressed against each other as close as Siamese twins. They were five and six years old, babies in a foreign place on a foreign day. They couldn't understand what was happening or even say that they were afraid. It was the tenth day of their first school year on an unfamiliar island in an unknown country. They had learned only a few words of English.

Norm Caswell had three sons. He was praying they were home, safe. He climbed into the bus and picked up a boy in each arm, and they joined the line of children. Even protected by the bus chassis, they were struggling to keep their footing.

From the edge of his farm, Joe Matoes squinted into the storm. He could just make out the line of children emerging from the shelter of the school bus. They braced themselves against the rush of wind. Water eddied around their legs. The younger children were up to their chests, hanging on to the hands they held, squeezing as tight as they could. If they began to cry, no one heard them over the screaming voice of the storm. They could not see where they were going, could not even see the other children in the line, just the one or two on either side.

The water of Mackerel Cove was surprisingly warm and dirty, worse than the worst seaweed day. All kinds of things were floating in it, as if the contents of the town dump had been emptied into the cove by mistake. Matoes strained through the murk and cutting wind to pick out his children. His daughter Dorothy's new red skirt and the yellow school bus were spots of color on the gray-black day. As he watched, the children stumbled toward the road and began to advance together. One step, maybe two.

If you sail the New England coast between Portsmouth, New Hampshire, and Boston, about midpoint in your journey you'll round Cape Ann and pass by Thacher's Woe and Avery's Fall, a small island and memorial of sorts to the first documented hurricane in American history.

The Great Colonial Hurricane struck New England in the summer of 1635 when Plymouth Plantation was fifteen years old and the Massachusetts Bay Colony was in its fifth year. It landed at daybreak in Narragansett Bay and swung east to pummel the Pilgrim settlements. Trees, houses, and wigwams fell. A merchant ship was tossed up on shore near Boston and at least eight people drowned. It was said that six hours of rage were followed by an eclipse of the moon.

In Boston, Governor John Winthrop wrote: "The wind caused the tide to rise to a height unknown before and drowned eight Indians flying from their wigwams."

Plymouth governor William Bradford described "such a mighty storm of wind and rain as none living in these parts, either English or Indian, ever saw. It began in the morning a little before day, and grew not by degrees but came with violence in the beginning, to the great amazement of many." He likened it to "those hurricanes and typhoons that writers make mention of in the Indies."

New England Puritans who witnessed its fury believed the Great Colonial Hurricane was a tempest of biblical proportion. They compared it to the Great Deluge and feared that the prophecies of the Apocalypse were coming to pass. The only storm they had seen approaching was a spiritual one, stirred by the radical preaching of the charismatic young cleric Roger Williams.

In the summer of 1635, the Plymouth and Boston colonies were thinly settled and struggling to gain a foothold in the New World. The Great Colonial Hurricane struck toward the end of the planting season. It disrupted harvesting and battered ships bringing new settlers and vital supplies. The four-hundred-ton *Great Hope*, out of Ipswich, England, was driven aground near Charlestown, not far from the spot where Paul Revere would wait, booted and spurred, more than a hundred years later, to spread the alarm.

The worst wreck, though, "one of the most disastrous that ever afflicted the iron-bound coast of New England," occurred on the short, usually uneventful sail from Ipswich to Marblehead. A pinnace carrying Anthony Thacher and John Avery, ministers and cousins, and their young families was dashed against a small rocky island off Cape Ann. The Reverend Thacher recounted the ordeal in a letter to his brother in Salisbury: "We were driven before the wind and waves, expecting with every wave to be swallowed up and drenched in the deeps. . . . Ghastly death every moment stared us in the face." The ship was lifted onto a stony ledge where "the violence of the wave and fury of the winds (by the Lord's permission) . . . beat her all to pieces."

Thacher, who could not swim a stroke, was "driven hither and thither in the seas a great while." Finally, like Jonah spit from the belly of the whale, he was thrown back onto the rock. Just beyond his grasp, he saw his daughter Mary, his cousin John Avery, and Avery's son struggling to reach him — "all three of them looking ruefully on me on the rock; their very countenances calling unto me to help them, who I could not go unto, neither could they come to me. Oh! I yet see their cheeks, poor silent lambs, pleading pity and help at my hands."

Near midnight, the Great Colonial Hurricane passed and the wind was silenced. Thacher waited and listened, hoping to hear his children calling. At first the night was blank. The only sound was the slap of the sea, then the scuttle of the pinnace cast ashore. Thacher found his wife entangled in the wreckage. For three days the couple stayed on the island rock, praying to be reunited with their children. The sea returned one body to them, and on the third day a passing shallop rescued them. From that day, the tiny island and treacherous rock off Cape Ann have been called Thacher's Woe and Avery's Fall, and the colonists built a lighthouse there to warn other ships of the peril.

In the years that followed, the story of Thacher's Woe was often told "about the hearth-fires of the coast-dwellers in the long winter evenings and the fishermen with 'grave and reverend' faces, recalled the ancient tale when they passed the fatal ledge and saw the white waves breaking over it."

Three hundred years later, another father, on another island off the New England coast, watched as his children were hurled into a hurricane sea. Like the Reverend Thacher, Joe Matoes was helpless to save them.

No one on the island of Jamestown had ever witnessed such a tumult in Mackerel Cove. Murderous winds screamed off the bay. They smacked the line of children holding hands on the causeway and pushed the empty school bus across the road into the water of Sheffield Cove. The sheltering arms of the cove hugged the rampaging sea, hemming it in, forcing it to rise until the storm surge was a liquid wall as solid as stone, as high as a house, higher than any wall the children had ever seen. Like a voracious giant, it picked up the three-story bathing pavilion and swallowed it whole, leaving only the stone steps behind. Then it swaggered across the causeway, devouring everything in its path — stones, seaweed, automobiles, book bags. A row of children holding hands in a once sheltering cove did not stand a chance against such a marauder.

Visibility was two hundred feet at most. But for one fraction of a second, the miasma of spray and sea and rain and salt cleared, and Joe Matoes glimpsed two of his daughters. A wall of water as wide as the cove was tearing toward them. It lifted them up onto the roof of the bus. He saw them clutching at the sleek surface, their faces distorted in terror, their mouths open in a silent scream. Then the storm closed over the cove. From its vast height, the surging sea crushed over them. It dashed them off the roof and sucked them down again.

Exactly what happened next has been debated and argued on the island ever since. The mayhem of the hurricane created a confusion of conjecture, blame, heartbreak, and anger. Although memories were fractured and time has not added clarity, when pieced together, the various accounts create a certain picture.

Clayton Chellis had a tight grip on his sister, Marion. There was never a day in his eleven years when Clayton was more than a few feet from the sea. He grew up diving off the rocks at the Beavertail light, a treacherous spot that he swam with ease. But a rugged eleven-year-old weighs maybe seventy-five or eighty pounds. One cubic yard of water weighs about three-quarters of a ton. When Clayton came through the wall of water, he was alone.

He must have tried to find his sister, but the cove was a boiling stew. Sucked into the roaring sea, he drifted with it, stunned, half-drowned, exhausted by its force. He gave himself up to the sea and rode with the rushing current past Fox Hill Farm and up the bay.

Norm Caswell probably had a hold of Constantine and John Gianitis. A running wall of water was sweeping toward them, spilling tons of water. Doubling a wave's height quadruples its energy; tripling a wave's height increases its energy nine times. Caswell lost the boys in the first surge of the sea. He surfaced and was sucked down a second and a third time. The boys were five and six years old, so small and light that the wind could have picked them up and carried them like dandelion pods.

For the Matoeses, home was so close. A few strokes and they would reach their father on the banks of the farm. If Joseph tried to yell to his sisters, the wind took the words out of his mouth and filled his throat with rain and spray, choking him. Eunice slipped from his grasp. He dove under the wreckage and reached her again. Holding her with one arm in a lifesaver's grip, the boy tried to get his bearings and find Theresa and Dotty. There were cows from the farm in the water, dead fish, and beach cabanas. In the one clear second, Joseph must have seen his sisters on the roof of the bus.

When the surging sea flung them off, he swam to them, dragging Eunice with him. Theresa and Dotty grabbed on to him, and he tried to swim, pulling his sisters home. The Matoeses were all strong swimmers. A lifetime on an island accessible only by boat and swimming becomes second nature. They knew not to fight the tide, but in that nightmare moment, hurled into a raging sea, beaten by debris, weighed down by clothes and shoes, lessons were forgotten. Theresa and Dotty flailed against the storm.

On the bank of Fox Hill Farm in the gathering night, Joe Matoes braced himself against the wind. The air was wet and salty. Salt water washed his face, stung his eyes, dripped from his chin, and clogged his throat. Matoes's tears and the ocean ran together.

CHAPTER 18

Cast Adrift

The two women lay on their stomachs, trying simultaneously to keep the roof balanced, the debris off their backs, and the child safely between them. The detritus churning in the water and flying through the air was as menacing as the sea. Harriet Moore had no idea how long she and Margaret had been hanging on to the fragment of roof. They had lost all sense of time and of the larger world. Reality was reduced to their single diminishing piece of rooftop and the boundless water. It seemed a lifetime ago that Harriet had the luxury to worry about something as trivial as living room curtains. Now her only thought was saving her daughter.

Little Mary Moore, who had been treated like precious porcelain every day since her adoption, kept her eyes squeezed shut to keep the salt water out and braved the wild ride without a whimper. The child had been immersed in the water so long that she was shivering uncontrollably. The waves were tremendous. If they survived them, Harriet was afraid they'd be dashed to pieces against the wreckage that had piled up along the shore.

All of a sudden Margaret started shouting, "A tree! A tree!" Sure enough, sticking up through the water just ahead of them was about three inches of cedar. Where there was a treetop, there must be land. Before they had a chance to figure out a plan or attempt a landing, their roof-raft split. Margaret washed away on one piece. Harriet lost hold of the other. With Mary in her arms, she slid off the splintered roof.

Somehow, probably through sheer willpower, she managed to gain her footing. The water was chest-high and clogged, and the breakers were slamming in hard and fast. Harriet had all she could do just to hold on to Mary. She could not make any headway toward shore. Several times the force of the surf knocked her down and tore Mary from her arms. Each time, Harriet shot to the surface in a panic, thinking she had lost her daughter; each time, she managed to reach the child in time. A single relentless purpose drove Harriet: to bring Mary to safety.

Inch by inch, with her daughter wrapped in her arms, Harriet fought her way ashore. Hoisting Mary up in front of her and climbing behind, a foot at a time, she picked her way over the mounds of wreckage. When they finally reached firm ground, Margaret was there, waiting and praying. The three had washed across Little Narragansett Bay to Osbrook Point, Connecticut. It was dark and cold. Their sodden clothes were clammy and they were so exhausted that they would have gladly lain down on the wet ground and closed their eyes. But Harriet was afraid Mary could not survive the night out in the open. They had come through so much. She could not lose her daughter now. No matter how tired and battered they were, they had to keep on going until they found shelter.

With Mary between them holding hands, Harriet and Margaret began to run. The child tried to keep up, but she was too exhausted to take another step. Mary stumbled and fell on her face. She lay motionless on the wet, rutted path. Harriet turned her daughter over. Mary's mouth was foaming and her eyes had rolled up into her head. All around them the wind shrieked through the trees like a gleeful witch who had cast an evil spell and was coming to collect her prize. Harriet was more frightened than she had been on the furious sea, but she did the only thing she could think of. She pounded Mary on the back, beating the child with her fists to revive her. Mary came to, vomiting salt water. Harriet and Margaret got her on her feet, and the three started out again, more slowly and even more determined.

Osbrook Point was wooded and inky black. Brambles and fallen trees blocked them in every direction. They could not find their way. They were beyond exhaustion, stone-cold, and getting nowhere. Still, Harriet pressed them on. A herd of sheep ran by, scaring them almost to death, yet cheering them, too. Where there were sheep, there must be people.

They went a few more steps when they saw a man with two women coming down the road toward them. Harriet's friends Violet Cottrell and Denise O'Brien had washed up on Osbrook Point, too. "That meeting was more than words can say," Violet tried to explain later. "Each of us thought we would never see the other again." The man with them was another Fort Road refugee, Jerry Shea, one of the carpenters who had been working on the Burkes' house.

I see sharks. Sharks are following us!

Geoffrey Moore was shouting. He was leaning so far over their attic-floor raft, he almost slipped off. A pair of hammerheads, one slightly ahead of the other, their fins like black triangular blades, were swimming aginst the flow. Either the scent of blood on the water had drawn them or the storm had carried them in and they were trying to stay alive. Titanic waves thrashed over the raft, pelting the Moores with the broken contents of their own home. They clung to their makeshift raft for dear life and prayed that the violent waters were not carrying them out to sea. Except for Geoffrey's shark alarm, the children were silent. They were concentrating on their father. When he gave the signal, the girls closed their mouths and held their breath until the next wave thundered over them.

At the height of the tempest above Aunt May's perpetual prayers, the Moores heard a familiar cackle — *Hello, Polly!* — and Cathy's pet parrot hopped a ride on the raft. Then just to their east, they glimpsed a familiar landmark, the Dennison's Rock buoy in the middle of Little Narragansett Bay. An immense wave of relief, stronger than anything the storm could hurl, washed over them. Instead of being carried to sea, as they had feared, the Moores were sailing across the bay. At nightfall the attic floor beached itself on tiny Barn Island in Connecticut, right beside Catherine Moore's bedroom bureau.

"I hopped off, dragging Cathy after me," she remembered. "The others followed like deer jumping over a wall. We had no shoes, of course, and the island was a mass of bull briers and blackberry vines. Geoffrey stepped on a nail the first thing." They had only seconds to get off the raft, and Aunt May lost her footing. She dropped into what seemed like a deep well of water. Geoffrey reached out and yanked her onto the shore.

On Barn Island, which isn't an island at all but a part of Connecticut, the Moores found a haystack sheltered by a stone wall, and there in the field beneath a sky full of stars they spent the night. The air was chill, and they shivered in their wet clothes.

Their teeth chattered and they tried to stomp their feet to warm up. Too tired for even that small exertion, they burrowed into the hay for warmth.

Catherine Moore described the night:

> At the bottom of the haystack there was a hollow place about six feet long and three feet deep. This Jeff called the women's dormitory. We pulled down hay in the front of this place, while the men scooped out another place a few feet away. They decided to take the two younger children with them. Andy took Margaret and kept her covered with

hay. Jim took care of Cathy, and Geoffrey took care of himself. He had no shirt, and I pitied him with that briery hay scratching his skin all night, but he had no complaint to make and was as helpful as could be.

Catherine, Aunt May, Anne, Nancy, and Loretta lay side by side in the haystack cubbyhole, listening for a familiar sound — the whirr of a motor, a voice calling. Every now and then they shouted together: *Helloooooooo!* On the trip across the bay, they could barely see one another. Now the night was so clear, they could see for miles. An eerie radiance glowed like a sunset in the distance. The fire in New London was burnishing the sky.

George Chase was an odd duck. That was about the kindest thing most people had to say about him. In 1938 he was sixty, and if you happened to find yourself downwind of him, you might think he had not washed in as many years. Few knew him, or knew where he came from. As far as most people could remember, he showed up one day at the Davis farm over in Stonington — a stocky man of few words, six feet tall with a grizzly tangled beard, who dressed in bib overalls and a slouch straw hat, regardless of the season. The Davis farm spread for hundreds of acres along the banks of the Pawcatuck River, which separates Stonington, Connecticut, from Westerly, Rhode Island. How Chase happened to stop at that place, which has been in the Davis family since colonial days, is unclear. Old Man Davis was something of a character himself. He hired Chase to do odd jobs — tend the hogs, feed the hens, and the like. In exchange, Davis built him a twelve-foot-square cabin in the woods. It was furnished with a stove, a table, and a wooden bed. Chase lived alone with a one-man cat. He raised yellow-eyed beans in a cleared patch behind the cabin and picked pails of blackberries, raspberries, and strawberries in the woods. Once a week he rode into town with Old Man Davis in the Model A Ford truck, sold his berries to the Victory Bakery, and bought cans of Strongheart to feed his cat.

Local children thought Chase was the bogeyman and hid their faces when he passed. Parents kept their children away from him. But everyone on the Davis farm knew that "Old George," though "kind of colorful," was a "darn good man" — honest, hardworking, and quite a baker. His specialties were blueberry pie, spice cake, and great big pans of gingerbread. John "Whit" Davis Jr. remembers the time he and a hired hand stopped by the cabin. Chase was just taking a pan of gingerbread out of the oven. He cut two generous slices. Whit was maybe eleven or twelve, and he wolfed down his cake. The hired hand took a couple of bites. "Mmmm," he said to Chase, "raisins. I like plenty of raisins in my gingerbread." Old George took his pipe out of his mouth. It was a battered pipe with a curved stem. The end was wrapped in string to fit firmly between his two remaining upper teeth. "Not raisins," he said. "Flies in the batter."

As Wednesday blackened, George Chase lit his stove and settled in with a bottle of something cheap and potent. Taunting wind tore through the woods, and booming gusts shook the cabin. Chase swilled the last of his whiskey. He was lighting his pipe when the most improbable thing occurred. Someone knocked on his door. While he was considering this odd turn of events, a man — bruised, half naked, and dripping wet — burst in, sputtering an outlandish tale. Napatree was in ruins. The bay was crammed with houses. Bodies were washing up on the Connecticut shore.

George Chase snorted at the unlikely story, picked up his kerosene lantern, and went out into the storm to see for himself. The first survivor he found was an elderly lady, weak and close to death. She was Jane Grey Stevenson, proprietor of the Watch Hill gift shop. Mrs. John Warner, a Fort Road neighbor who rode across the bay on a door, was struggling to help her pick her way through the rubble on the shore.

Old George brought the women back to his cabin. "Mr. Chase gave me a cup of hot ginger tea, which burned all the way down but made me feel warm and alive," Jane Grey Stevenson recalled. "Then he gave me his overcoat and made me take off all my wet clothes, which he hung on a line over the stove.

"Some other survivors came, men and women, about six or eight, I think, and they all got the same good care. No praise can be too great for Mr. Chase's warm sympathy to all of us in that little house, just built to hold himself, his cot, and his stove."

By the time he finished gathering the shipwrecked refugees from Napatree, Chase had eleven wet, filthy, battered, exhausted, and grateful guests in his twelve-foot-square cabin. Besides Jane Grey Stevenson and Mrs. Warner, there were the three carpenters from the Burke house; the caretaker Herb Greenman; and Harriet Moore and her daughter, Mary; her maid, Margaret Kane; and her friends Violet Cottrell and Denise O'Brien. Chase was not used to company and he had no food to offer, but he kept the wood fire burning and shared what he had — ginger tea, milk, and a pail of stale water.

Harriet Moore described the odd scene: "The cabin was just about a one-room job and to fit us all in, it was necessary to do no moving when we were once seated. There were three on the bed, two on the floor, two on the wood box, three on the backless stools, and Mary in one of the carpenter's laps — just like peas in a pod. The host of the evening was most cordial in his own little way."

When the storm ceased and the sky cleared, Chase walked through the woods and knocked on Old Man Davis's kitchen door. With the fallen trees, the deep ponds, the heaps of rubble, and the darkness, it took a couple of hours to get to the main house and back, but about midnight he returned. John Davis followed on horseback with a loaf of bread and a bottle of apple cider or whiskey, memories vary.

While the refugees were waiting in Chase's rude cabin, Herb Greenman told the story of the rag doll that had given him courage. Harriet Moore recognized the doll from his description. It belonged to Mary. Sometime during the clean-up period, the rag doll turned up in the bathtub full of sand and seaweed. Harriet gave it to Greenman, who named it Hurricane Sue.

After the Great Hurricane blew through New England, George Chase's kitchen was never empty again. The unlikely hero who had sheltered fifteen or more refugees from the storm enjoyed a brief measure of local fame. As the attention faded and the survivors reordered their lives, Chase was forgotten by all except Harriet Moore.

Whit Davis, who was fourteen in 1938, remembers her visits: "She'd come down that road in her big limousine, with her chauffeur driving — and the road wasn't paved at that time. She'd bring food to George — you should have seen that food — and she did it for six years."

Chase died on December 1, 1944, as he had lived — alone and in poverty. But he is buried in the Stonington Cemetery beneath a handsome granite cross, inscribed with his name. As long as Harriet Moore lived, his grave was maintained with care.

Sometime after nine o'clock, four figures ventured out of the old fort at Napatree Point. Lillian, Jack, and the clammers stepped into a clear, pitch-black night and a place they had never seen before. The looming shadow in the far distance must be Watch

Hill. Pinpoints of light danced around it like fireflies. Otherwise, there were no lights except the stars — huge stars, as big and bright as moons.

They began to stumble down the beach, as uncertain and disoriented as Rip Van Winkle awakening after a hundred-year sleep. The beach was as clean as a whistle. Not a sign of the road they had driven. Not a car. Not a house. Not a chunk of seawall. Not a shingle. Not a clothespin. Thirty-nine houses washed away like sand castles. A summer idyll gone without a trace.

Lillian, Jack, and the clammers were the only four to survive the storm on Napatree. Fifteen people died there on September 21. Jane Grey's sister, Mary Stevenson, and their beloved maid, Elliefair Price, were drowned. Jim Nestor's aunt was found still clutching her overnight case. Her two maids drowned as well. Frank Pasetti, Herb Greenman's assistant, and Havila and Jessie Moore, who had been enjoying the spectacle of the storm from their glassed-in porch, were also lost. The letter that Jessie Moore gave to the postman that Wednesday was delivered long after her body was recovered. It was postmarked Watch Hill Station, Sept. 21, 4 P.M. Her husband, Fred, carried it in his wallet for the rest of his life.

Lillian and Jack married within a year. Their son, Jack Jr., said, "If they could weather the 'thirty-eight hurricane together, they believed they could go through anything."

Out at the southernmost tip of Beavertail on the island of Jamestown, churning water — half sand, half sea, the dirty yellow color of a mongrel dog — had been boiling up from the depths of the ocean and smashing against the lighthouse. Waves had broken over the granite tower and ripped out the side of the keeper's house, exposing the original 1749 foundation.

Carl and Ethel Chellis had spent the storm frantic with worry. Their eldest son, Bill, made it home, but Clayton and Marion were not back from school. Carl had tried to reassure his wife. The teacher was probably keeping the kids in school until the storm blew over. They were safer there. The lighthouse was a dangerous place to be in a vicious storm. Ethel was clinging to that reassuring thought when a car drove up to the lighthouse and the Chellises learned that their children were not safe in school.

Carl raced down to the cove. It was empty. There was no beach, no causeway, only a single body of water and the half-submerged school bus. Thinking there was a chance to save the children, Chellis dove into Sheffield Cove again and again. He did not know then that the bus was empty. Later in the evening, sometime between eight and nine o'clock, lights began moving around the head of Mackerel Cove. Although bathhouses were floating in the bay, most islanders didn't realize until the next morning that the lights in the cove came from searchers looking for the lost children. Along every beach on the Rhode Island shore, clusters of beams jumped and darted.

In the tons of wreckage, in the salt ponds and bay waters lapping docilely again as if nothing terrible and extraordinary had occurred within their banks, the search for the missing was under way. It started as soon as the sea retreated, and continued through the night and for days and weeks to come.

Along the South County shore, beacons flashing on Block Island were mistaken for distress signals from Charlestown and Misquamicut. Searchers waded out to the beaches with flashlights. What they found was stunning: "Not a vestige of any habitation was left, not even a foundation of any cottage. All that could be seen was a bare flat stretch of sand."

More than fifty bodies were recovered from Charlestown Beach that first night — neighbors and friends, entire families lost in an unguarded hour. The corpses were lined up on the sand for identification, and a makeshift morgue was set up in the high school in Westerly.

Timothy Mee of Charlestown Beach, whose wife and two little children were torn from his arms, described the harrowing moments: "I was tossed about beneath the water and kept going down and down and down. Then I started to come to the surface. It seemed an eternity. When I reached the top, I looked around, and there was no one in sight. Debris struck at me from all sides as I was hurled wildly along with the waves. Finally, I landed on the shore of Green Hill Pond. I staggered to my feet but the force of the wind knocked me down time and time again.

"Shortly afterward, I saw my dog Buster, swimming for the shore with our maid holding on to his collar. She was badly bruised, but safe. My wife, children, and companions were all lost. My car is in the pond. It can stay there. I never want to see Charlestown Beach again."

For days after the hurricane, Mee stayed in the makeshift morgue at Charlestown day and night. The Red Cross workers could not get him to leave. He viewed every body that came in, looking for his wife and children. Only the body of baby Jean was recovered.

September 21, 1938, was New England's darkest night. The Northeast coast was as black as mourning. From Long Island to Cape Cod, candles, like tentative rays of hope, flickered in windows in the suddenly silent night. Once the manic roar of the hurricane ceased, the silence seemed intrusive, the absence of sound itself a voice that demanded attention. After the storm's incessant din, the silence was unexpected and unearthly.

In the predawn hours, the Great New England Hurricane crossed the border into Canada. The three-thousand-mile marathon that had begun twelve days before in the tropical sea off northwest Africa petered out in the chilly northern latitudes at 2 A.M. Thursday morning. The Hurricane of 1938 had made the final leg of its trip — the surprising sprint from the Carolinas to Canada — in a single day. When it staggered into Montreal, it was still blowing at gale force.

Throughout the devastated areas, there was a surreal quality to those predawn hours. Deer and elk bounded from their cages and roamed Roger Williams Park in Providence. In Newport, lobsters by the thousands escaped from broken traps and swam down Thames Street, so many that the street looked like a massive lobster tank. A river in Massachusetts flowed with tapioca from an adjacent pudding factory, and at East Hampton's posh Maidstone Club, the swimming pool was crowded with bluefish and striped bass.

Dazed survivors wandered the beaches. They haunted hospitals and makeshift morgues, looking for missing family and neighbors. "It felt just as though you'd been through hell and back again," one said. Others were scavenging. As the waters ebbed, hordes of looters flooded in. At the beaches, they cut fingers off corpses to steal the rings. In the towns, they cleaned out stores.

From his vantage point in downtown Providence, author David Cornel de Jong watched the looters descend:

> They came neck deep or swimming, holding flashlights over their heads, rising out of the water and disappearing through demolished store windows. Hordes assisting each other piled goods into rowboats or stuffed them into burlap bags. They seemed organized, almost regimented,

as if they had daily drilled and prepared for this event the like of which had not happened in one hundred twenty years. They were brazen and insatiable; they swarmed like rats; they took everything. When a few policemen came by in a rowboat, they did not stop their looting. They knew they outnumbered the police; besides the latter were intent on rescue work.

The National Guard was called out. By midnight, Providence looked like a city in wartime. Armed soldiers patrolled the streets, and antiaircraft lights illuminated the night. Looting was so rampant throughout the state that Rhode Island remained under martial law for weeks, and National Guardsmen were ordered: "shoot to kill."

CHAPTER 19

All Quiet

Hard rain was bouncing off the glass dome of the old Pennsylvania Station and sliding down its steel ribs when Tot Greene's husband, Norvin, caught the train to the Hamptons about two o'clock, as he did every summer Wednesday. The weather was miserable and getting worse, but the train left on time. Wind and rain played a steady beat against the windows. Greene settled in with the day's papers. He had saved the morning *Times* and *Herald Tribune* to read on the train. The headlines in both were grim: more saber rattling in Europe.

The *Trib* had a glowing review of David Cornel de Jong's new novel. Greene might have glanced at it, thinking that Tot would enjoy the book. On the editorial page of the *Times* there was a brief item slugged HURRICANE:

The hurricane that happily spared our southern shore struck terror into the hearts of Floridians and reminded even the far-away New Yorkers that nature is not to be

trifled with when she is in one of her angrier moods. If
New York and the rest of the world have been as well
informed about the cyclone, it is because of an admirably
organized meteorological service.

Greene may have read the editorial and then dozed off. The
next thing he knew, the train was jerking to a stop. The crew ran
through the cars, cracking open the emergency cases and grabbing axes and saws. The hurricane "that had happily spared our
southern shore" had reached Long Island, and a tree was block-
ing the tracks just outside of Manorville. It took an hour to clear.
By then, the wind and rain were torrential. The train continued
as far as Speonk, about fifteen minutes from Westhampton, and
stopped again. The tracks ahead were washed out. One train had
already derailed.

In the furious gale, Norv Greene had one thought — to reach
his family on Dune Road in Westhampton Beach any way he
could. When the train could go no farther, he hired a cab. When
the road became impassable, he got out and walked. About nine
o'clock, he reached Quogue, one town away from Westhampton,
and learned that there was no more Dune Road. Like Fort Road
on Napatree, the hurricane had wiped it clean. What bridges
there had been were down, and breachways had opened, turning
Westhampton Beach into a strand of islands.

Greene was directed to Quogue's Patio Restaurant, where an
emergency police station had been set up. It consisted of a chair
and a table. On the table were a lined yellow pad with the names
of the survivors and a candle to read them by. No Greenes were
listed. Norv went into the bar for a drink. There was no water
because the mains had burst, but there were plenty of bottled
drinks. He was ordering when he heard from the other end of the

bar ". . . and that lovely Mrs. Greene with her two children, all washed out to sea."

The hurricane in Long Island had ended by 5:30 P.M., less than three hours after it landed. The search for the missing and dead began immediately. As the victims were recovered, they were brought to the Westhampton Country Club and lined up on the floor of the ballroom, where many of them had danced over the Labor Day weekend. Norv did not go to the club Wednesday night. "I couldn't face it if they were there," he said.

The only way to reach Dune Road — or what was left of it — was by boat, but locating a boat that could still float was a challenge. The Coast Guard took cutters from the Battery, loaded them onto trucks, and drove through the night, navigating the obstacle course from Manhattan to the Hamptons. When the first rescue boat set out at dawn, Norv Greene was on board. He saw a small bedraggled group struggling toward the bay, carrying a crippled man on a wooden door. The Schmid group had been found.

Annie Seeley, the Schmids' maid, drowned in the hurricane, but her desperate phone call very likely saved the lives of Mona and Joan. If they had not tried to reach Annie, in all probability they would have died, too. Peggy Connolly Brown, the friend they had been visiting, was lost with her baby. Rather than let go of the child's body to save herself, mother and child drowned together. The baby was never found. The friend in the house across the road who called to Mona and Joan to come in out of the storm also died with her mother.

The Coast Guard brought the bedraggled survivors back to Westhampton Village, where one young admirer bought the Schmid sisters their first shot of whiskey. Another flew to their rescue from Yale. When he landed in Westhampton, he scooped up the girls, told them they looked awful, and ushered them into the drugstore to buy a comb and lipstick.

Although they had never been susceptible before, both Mona and Joan were covered with severe poison ivy and oak. It must have been carried on the wind, and the force of the gale embedded the poison in their bodies. They were sick for almost three weeks. Everything they owned — including their clothes, from underwear to outerwear — was gone. Their mother telephoned B. Altman, where they often shopped. The store knew their sizes and hand-delivered everything to their Brooklyn Heights apartment. "We were B. Altman people to the bitter end," Mona said. The genteel Fifth Avenue department store closed in the 1980s.

The Schmids did not return to Westhampton. Joan married and lived in Islip, but for Mona, "the hurricane was the end of my Long Island era." Sixty-five years later, she has never been back to Westhampton Beach.

Once they had deposited the Schmids safely, Norv Greene and the rescue party crept out again. The wreckage in the water made for rough going. The biggest worry was the fallen telephone wires. If they tangled in the propellers, the boats would be useless. As the cutter moved slowly along the shore, the small hope that Greene had clung to faded. Westhampton Beach was a wasteland. The occasional house still standing was not much more than a shell. Finally, he recognized his own battered home. Jumping over the side of the boat, he waded to the beach. There, walking through the sand toward him, looking as if they had stepped out of the pages of *Robinson Crusoe*, were his wife, Tot; his children, Gretchen and Gair; and maybe a dozen others.

The Greene family and the neighbors they had sheltered had

waited out the end of the hurricane in their precarious attic room. But Tot was afraid the house would fall if another monstrous wave came in on the evening tide. When the storm quieted, she fed the children bread with ketchup, which was the only food she could salvage, then she and her "houseguests" wandered through the desolation of Westhampton Beach, looking for a more substantial shelter to spend the night. The shore was a snarl of debris — downed power lines, shifting sands, and ruined homes. The men carried the children piggyback, picking their way cautiously in the twilight.

About a quarter of a mile down the beach, they came to one of the few houses still standing. It was built of concrete and stone and was closed for the season. The men broke in and built a fire, burning books and furniture because the logs in the cellar were saturated. Tot couldn't find any blankets, so she took down some curtains, wrapped the children in them, and bundled them all into one big bed. Pat Driver, one of the children at the Greenes' end-of-summer party, remembers lying "side by side for warmth, shivering and still terribly frightened."

Once they were safe in the village, the Greenes read the morning headlines: BROKER'S WIFE AND CHILDREN'S BIRTHDAY PARTY SWEPT OUT TO SEA. The story in the *New York Sun* said, "The names of many children appeared on the missing list after the home of Mrs. Norvin Greene, who was giving a party for her two children, was swept away in the deluge. Not a single member of the gathering at the party was seen again."

When the sun rose Thursday morning, the Moores saw for the first time what a wreck they were — muddied clothes; clotted, bedraggled hair stuck with hay; faces blackened with grime; legs bruised and scraped. Jeff's woolen shirt had shrunk to half its size, so it looked like a bolero. Four-year-old Margaret, the only one who had no trouble sleeping, woke up and asked, "What's for breakfast, Mummy?"

Catherine laughed. "Help yourself to a little hay, darling."

Geoffrey, whose bare chest was crosshatched with scratches, found a mirror in the wreckage and as the sun brightened, he began sending signals. In no time, the refugees spotted a trawler. Calling and shouting, they picked their way down to the shore. Thorns and splinters pierced their bare feet, and they stepped gingerly. Old Mr. Scott, a lobster vendor from the nearby town of Avondale, was nosing his boat through the rubble. "If it had been the most palatial yacht ever to sail the seven seas," Catherine Moore said, "it couldn't have looked more beautiful that morning."

Scott had to lower a dinghy because his lobster boat could not maneuver close enough through the shallow, wreck-filled water to reach them. It took three trips to ferry all ten. Once they were safely on deck, the Moores looked out on the empty beach that yesterday had been Napatree. Nothing remained except the old fort.

"We glanced over the bay at the place we had loved so much, the place we had often called Heaven on Earth," Catherine said. "It just wasn't there. A strip of sand and a few telephone poles were all that remained to mark the place that was known as the Fort Road."

CHAPTER 20

The Reckoning

Thursday, September 22, was another perfect day. The sun was warm, the water sparkled, and the sea was back in its bed. Everywhere else was desolation. People woke up to an unfamiliar landscape. Nothing looked the same. Streets they had walked all their lives and beaches where they had learned to swim and had taught their children to swim were unrecognizable. Harbors, normally crowded with boats, were empty lakes that glistened in the sunshine. Main Streets were marinas. Boats were everywhere except at their moorings. Yachts, trawlers, sloops, barges, were beached on village greens, in backyards, on front porches, across railroad tracks. One Long Island family who lived three-quarters of a mile from any navigable water woke up Thursday morning to find five fair-size boats in the backyard.

Roadways were sand dunes. Entire communities were stacks of kindling. The few telephone poles still standing were clotheslines, their crossbars hung with blankets, ribbons of seaweed, and clothing. Bonfires burned on the beaches to clean up the mess.

Landmarks that had stood long before anyone could remember had vanished, and along the shores of ponds and bays, white muslin flags, each with a red cross, fluttered in the light breeze. Every flag marked the location of a body to be picked up.

Although houses broke up, much of their furnishings stayed intact, and on Thursday the coastline looked like a vast yard sale. Along the edges of salt ponds and marshes, in pastures and fields, there were chairs and tables and tennis racquets, bureaus and refrigerators.

A Westhampton woman said the scene Thursday morning defied description. "Devastation everywhere, debris, smelly mud, furniture, cars, lumber and big chunks of houses, boats, trees, all jumbled and tangled in mountainous heaps, and scattered everywhere. Yachts stuck in hedges, buildings broken and twisted, the dunes flattened, almost devoid of the beautiful summer cottages we took such pride in, and ocean waves breaking in the bay where the inlets had broken through the dunes. It was all but impossible to comprehend such devastation, let alone figure out how to begin to clean it up."

What the eye saw, the mind could not process and the heart refused to accept. The reality of this morning seemed disconnected from the memory of yesterday morning. Even the birds seemed disoriented. One Rhode Island man said, "They came out — what birds were left — but they seemed spooky. They were as still as could be. They didn't sing or anything." Another man said: "They were flying around in groups as if they were thinking of migrating." A gannet, an ocean bird whose habitat is the North Atlantic, and tropical yellow-billed birds native to the West Indies were spotted in Vermont.

The hurricane turned back the clock to a time when homes were lit by candlelight, meals were cooked in the fireplace, and walking was the most reliable mode of travel. Much of Connecticut and Massachusetts and all of Rhode Island were marooned. Transportation did not exist. Five Massachusetts Supreme Court judges who had set out from Springfield to Boston, a distance of one hundred miles, on Wednesday morning finally arrived in a National Guard truck convoy Friday night.

Without power or phone lines, even neighboring towns were cut off from each other. It was days before the scope of the disaster was understood. In much of the stricken area, the only communication with the outside world was by shortwave radio. Amateur hams Wilson Burgess and George Marshall radioed from Westerly, signaling the Red Cross for disaster relief, the State House for soldiers, and the utility companies for linemen. They stayed at their radio through the night and received the William S. Paley Amateur Radio Award for their efforts.

Driving was hazardous. Roads were buried beneath sand or blocked by trees and debris. Without electricity, service stations could not pump gas. Train service was derailed completely. The New York, New Haven & Hartford Railroad reported that "seventy-five miles of silent track hung at crazy angles over yawning chasms, in a hopeless jumble of power lines, signal towers, houses, boats and thousands of tons of debris." Thirty-one bridges and two hundred culverts were washed out, moved from their abutments or demolished. Five thousand men worked in shifts twenty-four hours a day, seven days a week, to restore service so that vital goods and relief supplies could get in. Many of the railroad workers ate and slept in the Pullman cars that had stalled on the tracks. In the meantime, the navy battleship USS *Wyoming* carried the mail between New York and Boston.

Telephone service was equally chaotic. According to Bell Telephone Company figures, more than 500,000 phones were dead in some 350 communities, major cable routes were destroyed, and so many miles of telephone, telegraph, and power lines were down they could stretch four-fifths of the way around the world. Seventy-two million feet of wire, 400 miles of cable, 31,000 poles, and 18,000 crossarms had to be replaced. Telephone workers streamed in from as far away as Nebraska. Urgent calls from New York and Washington were routed by undersea cable to London and then relayed back across the Atlantic to wireless stations on eastern Cape Cod.

The weather remained glorious for the rest of September. "Everything was beautifully clean after that," one man remembered. "The next day and the next few weeks you never saw the air so clean. At night, you could see stars you never could see before. It made me respect nature a heck of a lot. In fact, I feel Mother Nature does that every once in a while — like washing an old dirty shirt." But the landscape was barren.

Autumn never came to New England in 1938. The region passed from summer to the bleakness of winter in a few hours. Trees were stripped bare. Vegetation was dead. The few sorry bits of verdure that remained were burned brown because the hurricane had rained salt water. Whatever green there was lay prostrate, a horizontal jungle of lost majesty — great maples, oaks, and elms, the pride of many colonial towns, fallen.

Trude Crombe of Rhode Island said, "Leaves weren't just blown off trees — the juices were sucked out of them like a vacuum cleaner would draw it right up." A Jamestown woman wrote to a friend: "Besides the tragic loss of life, homes and property, much of the beauty of the island is gone. The coast line stands stark and naked." A Long Island woman wrote to her mother:

"We are having beautiful weather and lovely moonlight nights, but in spite of that, the place seems dead."

In the country, the odor of crushed foliage filled the air. Trees that had held against the storm stood like remnants of a lost battalion. Along the beaches and in the flooded cities, the stench of rotting sea creatures and sewage was revolting. Pedestrians in downtown Providence shared the sidewalk with rats as big as tomcats. Food and water sources were contaminated. Cars and corpses filled coves, ponds, and bays. In farms across New England, chickens fluttered featherless wings. The wind had plucked them clean. Salt and sap were everywhere, clouding windows, sticking to walls, corroding cars. Copper screens turned green.

"It was easy to trace the boundary line where the storm surge had stopped," Lee Davis, the Westhampton doctor's son, recalled. "Oceanward from it, everything was coated with a dark, almost lavender layer of silt, a combination of sand and bay mud, plastered together and then blasted onto the surface of grass, shrubs, wreckage, homes, cars. There was death everywhere — of people, of comfort, of predictability, of yesterday. Nothing would ever return to the way it had been a mere morning ago."

In the face of such devastation, cleaning up, rebuilding, and starting over seemed insurmountable tasks. President Roosevelt dispatched 100,000 relief workers from the WPA, Civilian Conservation Corps, army, and Coast Guard. Boy Scouts and volunteers joined relief workers from the Red Cross. (Some Red Cross teams were delayed because they had been transferred to Florida when the hurricane threatened the southern coast.)

There was a run on axes and shingles. The sound of saws day and night replaced the voice of the wind. After so many years of depression, unemployment ended overnight. There was enough cleanup work for everyone.

In the wake of the storm, reporters descended on the D.C. Weather Bureau looking for answers, and letters — some angry, some perplexed — poured in. Gordon Dunn fired off a report to the Weather Bureau chief defending Jacksonville's actions. "If the hurricane had maintained its west-northwest course, it would have found Florida prepared as never before," he noted. "Warnings issued for the North Carolina coast were timely and accurate."

From Long Island, Ernest Clowes, the amateur weather watcher, sent a furious letter to Washington protesting "the total lack of warnings." "No one remembers such a wreck here. Yet our forecast was just gale warnings such as happen maybe half a dozen times every winter." John Q. Stewart, a Princeton physicist who was in northern New England when the hurricane struck, wrote in *Harper's* magazine: "In the long and laudable annals of the government's forecasters, that day's record makes what must be the sorriest page. There had been no warning worth the mentioning: telephones and coast guards were scarcely called to service. A sophisticated population died by the hundreds with little or no knowledge of what raw shape of death this was which struck from the sky and the tide."

The Weather Bureau countered by pointing out that it had issued seventeen warnings and that in twelve of them, the storm was designated a hurricane. The Bureau failed to note that virtually all twelve had emanated from Jacksonville. Defending Washington's performance, C. C. Clark, acting director there, blamed the extraordinary velocity of the storm. Once it left Cape Hatteras, the hurricane tripled its speed, dashing six hundred miles in twelve hours. In a response to Ernest Clowes's letter, Clark wrote: "Had the storm not moved with such unprecedented

rapidity, there can be no doubt but that Weather Bureau warnings by radio and through the press would have reached nearly
everyone in the affected area."

Unappeased, Clowes dispatched a second adamant letter: "It
seems to me that the whole virtue of good forecasting is not
merely to predict the obvious but to predict the exceptional. This
was an exceptional storm [and it] called for exceptional rather
than somewhat routine assumptions, judgment, and decisions."
Clowes blamed senior D.C. forecasters for the failure, among
them "my good friend Mr. Mitchell."

While publicly the Weather Bureau insisted it was blameless,
behind the scenes a major shake-up was under way. In an effort
"to greatly strengthen" the agency, F. W. Reichelderfer, a navy
commander with a take-no-prisoners attitude, was appointed chief.
Carl G. A. Rossby, a noted meteorologist at MIT, was brought in
as assistant chief, a new position, and given a mandate to develop
a research and training program. Charles Pierce, the only forecaster to recognize the danger, received a promotion and was
moved to the analysis division. He remained with the Weather
Bureau (now the National Weather Service) for the rest of his
career.

The shake-up did not still the storm of controversy inside or
outside the Weather Bureau. In the D.C. station, fourteen frus-
trated forecasters signed their own reorganization plan and pre-
sented it to the new chief. The signatories wrote: "This plan of
reorganization of the Forecast Room is based on a conception of
the forecaster as a scientist, executing a scientific duty or working
on a scientific problem — namely forecasting of weather." They
urged that "the Forecast Room in the interest of morale and effi-
ciency should be considered and administered as a scientific laboratory."

The most scathing critique of all came from Gardner Emmons, assistant professor of meteorology at New York University, meteorologist at Woods Hole Oceanographic Institute, and co-author of the January memorandum on the need to modernize the Bureau. Writing in *The Collecting Net* (a meteorological journal) in March of 1939, he charged that the deadly storm surge could have been predicted. Emmons criticized Jacksonville for assuming that the storm would curve to the northeast. Given the placement of the Bermuda High, he argued, "It is difficult to see how the storm could have been expected to veer out to sea off Hatteras. It would have been more logical to anticipate a movement straight up the Atlantic Coast." Emmons directed his sharpest words at Washington. "No advices to interested parties to stand by for possible hurricane warnings were given out, as was done earlier in the week by the Jacksonville forecast center." Referring to Charles Mitchell, he concluded: "Perhaps the most amazing aspect of the whole affair is that the official forecaster who made this seemingly inexcusable error of judgment is beyond all doubts the best forecaster at the Washington forecast center, if not the best in the entire Weather Bureau. How can his disastrous failure to make a timely and correct diagnosis be accounted for?"

Commander Reichelderfer circulated Emmons's article among the senior forecasters, asking for their comments. Mitchell scrawled in answer, "Mr. Emmons went off half-cocked it seems to me."

Sixty-five years later, defenses, accusations, explanations, and analyses of the missed forecast are still being made. But no matter which side you come down on, the shortest and truest answer is that the Great New England Hurricane simply outran the forecasters. It was too fast for the men in the Weather Bureau and the limited resources they had in 1938. As a result, 682 people died and another 1,754 were seriously injured.

Maine was the only New England state without a fatality. Eighty-eight died in Massachusetts, ninety in Connecticut, twelve in New Hampshire, and seven in Vermont. One person drowned in New York City, a hitchhiker in Queens who tried to swim away after the car that picked him up stalled. More than fifty died on Long Island, including twenty-nine in the Westhampton Beach area. "It was a great relief to find friends who had survived," Mona Schmid remembered. "There were so many funerals — every day a funeral, and Long Island was nothing compared with Rhode Island."

More than half of the dead — 433 — were in Rhode Island, the greatest toll along the beaches of South County. Nancy Allen Holst, a forest ranger, Red Cross volunteer, and pilot, flew her plane along the shoreline because it was easier to see the bodies from the air. Many people had put on their boots to slog through the water, she explained. The boots filled with water and weighed the bodies down so that only the tops of their heads were visible. When Holst spotted a corpse, she zoomed down, and a boat would go out to retrieve it.

Herbert Rathbun, just out of Dartmouth in June, was the official coroner for the Westerly area. In the wake of the hurricane, the town council informed him, "Somebody's got to collect the bodies and you're it."

"We usually brought the bodies in on a door," Rathbun recalled. "I laid them out in rows on the high school floor and tied a tag around the wrist or ankle." The governor dispatched undertakers to South County so embalming could keep pace with the discovery of corpses. Still there was a shortage of caskets and embalming fluid.

Lists of the dead and missing were continually revised, and the search became grimmer with each day that passed. Sometimes an arm or leg led to a body. Sometimes a smell. Sometimes the sea-gulls. If the birds located a body first, identification became excruciating. One ship's captain was identified from a hardware store receipt in his pocket. Many bodies were never found.

"No one was untouched," Arthur Raynor of Long Island said. "Everybody lost something; many, someone."

When the bay retreated at Mackerel Cove in Jamestown, the school bus stood beaten, abandoned, and half submerged, the water splashing quietly against it. The entire town walked down to the cove to see it. According to those who remembered the sight, the bus doors were shut, the windows were unbroken, and the interior was perfectly dry. There had been nine on the school bus when it started across the causeway. Two survived — eleven-year-old Clayton Chellis and the driver, Norm Caswell.

Jamestown had never known a tragedy to equal this one. The island was a small town. Everyone knew everyone. As volunteers combed fields, roads, and shoreline, the sea gave back the children, one by one. Theresa Matoes was recovered Thursday night. Her body was washed home onto the banks of Fox Hill Farm. Her brother, Joseph, was found the next morning, a quarter of a mile north of the cove. They were buried together from the Portuguese church in Newport. The following Tuesday, Marion Chellis was recovered about a mile and a half north, and Constantine Gianitis was found at Watson Farm, near the beach pavilion roof. His brother, John, washed up on the beach a short distance from the school bus. A week after the storm the remains of Eunice, the youngest Matoes, were discovered on the west shore of Beavertail. She was identified by the baby ring on her finger. All the children were found except ten-year-old Dotty Matoes.

"God keeps one for every three he returns," her cousin Marge Matoes Moran said. "It is an old belief."

Dorothy Matoes was listed missing and presumed dead. One morning, after the search for her body had finally been abandoned, Ethel Chellis looked out the window of the Beavertail lighthouse and spotted something in the bay. She thought it was a red-and-white lobster buoy, until she trained her husband's binoculars on the sight. Dotty's new red skirt and white blouse came into focus.

By then, the Gianitises had fled from Jamestown. They buried their boys and left as suddenly and as quietly as they had arrived. Joe Matoes continued to lease the pastures of Fox Hill Farm, and Carl and Ethel Chellis stayed on at the Beavertail light. Four years later they had another child, a son whom they named Richard.

The debate over the school bus tragedy continued for years. To this day, some on the island say that Norman Caswell made a fatal choice. The children would have been safe if he had kept them on the bus and sat out the storm. Others believe they would have drowned when the bus was swept into the cove. In the days and weeks that followed, dozens of conflicting versions of the tragedy were related, repeated, and argued over.

The version given here is the most plausible scenario. But it is in part conjecture. There were three witnesses — Norman Caswell, Joe Matoes Sr., and Clayton Chellis. Each had a different memory.

The day after the hurricane, a distraught Caswell told his story to a reporter from the *Providence Evening Bulletin:*

I never dreamed it could be so bad. The wind was kicking
up some when I started across the beach with the bus, but

even when I became stalled with the rest of the motorists, I didn't think the danger was so great. Some of the people in the first cars got out and said they would go for help. They never came back.

As we were sitting there, the wind got worse, and then a big wave came and broke right over the roof of the bus. Then a second wave came and I decided we'd better get out or we'd drown like rats. I ran to the rear of the bus, opened the door, and told the kids to join hands. I don't know exactly what happened after that. I know I held onto the hands of two of the kids and something struck. I went down three times, and when I came up the third time, I didn't have them anymore. They had been screaming but now I heard nothing.

I saw Clayton Chellis swimming around, then I lost him. I saw little Joe Matoes, too. He was going after his sister and the poor kid drowned in the attempt. He had plenty of spunk.

I was awfully tired with my wet clothes dragging me down, but I managed somehow to land on the end of Fox Hill where I pulled myself from the water by the grass. I laid there and in a minute the water came and covered me up. I struggled up again and saw young Chellis. The kid had made it. I told him to run to the Matoes' farm. I saw Matoes come down to help me but he couldn't find me and I couldn't yell loud enough to have him hear me. Finally, I struggled up and hung over the bars of a fence where they found me.

I still had my watch when I arrived at Matoes' house and it was stopped at 5:35 P.M. I guess that must have been the time the big wave hit us.

Some thirty-five years later, Joe Matoes gave a different account to Everett Allen, a New Bedford newspaperman:

In the afternoon, I got to listening on the radio about a storm coming. So, I started for the schoolhouse for my kids. They had already left on the bus, so I started to come back and when I hit the beach, the water was about four feet high. At Mackerel Cove, the waves were getting worse and worse, the wind was getting stronger, and pretty soon the pavilion went just like that, and the water was so high that my car and two others were swept into the water. I jumped overboard, my car was in a deep spot right near the cemetery, and I got ashore along a stonewall, all soaking wet.

There was a woman and a boy in a car and she drove down the hill and they were washed overboard, too, and both drowned. I was still by the wall; I saw Norman Caswell coming around the bend with the bus, and I waved him back. I don't know if he saw me or not. I saw the school bus go over — with the kids. Caswell opened the doors, and let the kids off. Well I had two daughters on top of the roof of the bus, screaming their heads off. I saw them get swept off.

I saw something coming through the water, something moving and stretched out, so I took a chance and went down from the wall to the water. I got knocked down twice because the wind was so strong, but when I got there it was Norman Caswell. He was lying on his stomach, so I took my boot and kicked him, you know, in the ribs. He grunted. Well, I said, he's still alive. He says, "Please let me die. I lost a whole bunch of the kids I had in the school bus. Everything's gone. Please don't move me. Let me die."

I picked him up and threw him on my shoulder, and I walked up the road to where there was a wall to divide the roads. I said, "You stay there until I get onto the other side and I'll take you into my house." I put him down on the wall and he just turned over and rolled off and I had to pick him up again. Then I took him into my house. He said, "Where's my bus?" I said, "Down there in the pond." I gave him some dry clothes and I changed myself. He stayed until nine o'clock. Then the tide went down and we went down and looked at the bus.

Clayton Chellis's brother Bill tells a third story. Chellis, a thirty-year navy man now retired in Florida, was a junior at Rogers High School in Newport in 1938. He caught the last ferry back to Jamestown, the same one that Joe Matoes took. Usually Bill waited at the dock for the school bus to pick him up, but on the day of the storm some friends drove by. "Hey, Bill, we're going up to the lighthouse to look at the surf," they called. "Want a ride?" Because of that chance meeting, Bill Chellis missed the fatal school bus trip, but this is the story Clayton told him:

"The bus started across the causeway. It was on the road behind the pavilion, when the water got so bad, it drowned out the engine." Bill is not sure whether the children were still inside the bus, but "the waves took the pavilion and the school bus. They pushed the bus about a third of a mile into the pond and rolled it over into the water. Clayton was a seal in the water. He let the waves carry him, and he landed about three miles up the beach, just south of where the bridge is today. When Clayton got his footing, he saw the driver, Norm Caswell, in the water, too, and pulled him out."

Given the split-second speed of events and the terror unfolding, it is understandable that memories differ. Some of the discrepancies are minor. According to Matoes, the stalled cars on the causeway were abandoned; Caswell refers to "the rest of the motorists." But each account raises the same basic question: Where was the school bus for two and a half hours? The Jamestown schools were about a mile from Mackerel Cove. Dismissal was at 2:45 P.M. No matter how atrocious the weather, it would not take better than two hours to drive that distance.

If we assume that Caswell had only the Beavertail group on the bus, then he could not have driven directly from school to Mackerel Cove, or he would have arrived at the causeway ahead of Joe Matoes. Therefore, we have to assume that Caswell drove to the harbor to pick up Bill Chellis. Not finding the boy waiting, he continued on to Mackerel Cove. We know that the bus left school on time, because it was gone when Joe Matoes arrived. This would put the hour of departure between 2:45 and 3:00. The bus would then have reached Mackerel Cove no later than four o'clock. An hour and a half would have elapsed between the time Matoes saw the bus approach and when Caswell's watch stopped. Surely given such a substantial block of time, a father as good and decent as Joe Matoes would have tried in some way to rescue his children.

Since he did not, it seems more plausible to suppose that Caswell piled all the children into the bus, made the north end run, then looped back to deliver the Beavertail kids. If this was the case, he would have reached Mackerel Cove as the hurricane was peaking. But Caswell said, "The wind was kicking up some when I started across the beach with the bus, but even when I became stalled with the rest of the motorists, I didn't think the danger was so great."

Caswell was a fisherman. He certainly would have recognized a serious storm if he bumped into one. And if he swung through town, thinking Bill Chellis would be waiting at the ferry, the bus would have gone down Conanicut Avenue, through water up to its hubcaps, and Caswell would have seen the destruction in the harbor.

No one will ever know exactly what happened. Norman Caswell never recovered from the school bus tragedy. He died a few years later, and his wife, Annie, took over the bus route.

Across the state in Westerly, Andy Pupillo, the Moores' handsome young handyman, never recovered from the hurricane, either. His sister blamed the Moores. She believed that Andy sustained internal injuries during the storm. The Moores believe that he was in the first stage of tuberculosis, an often fatal disease before streptomycin. Exposure in the hurricane and the chill night on Barn Island may have aggravated the TB. Andy's condition deteriorated rapidly. He died within a year, at the age of twenty-two.

Jeff Moore was booked on a flight to Chicago in 1939. He was running late and arrived at the airport gate as the plane was taxiing down the runway. The flight crashed. There were no survivors. The next year Jeff went into the hospital for surgery. He died there of an embolism at the age of forty. Catherine Moore raised their four children alone. She never remarried.

Harriet and Cy Moore adopted a second girl, then had twin daughters of their own. When Mary grew up and married, she adopted three children.

CHAPTER 21

The Last of the Old New England Summers

Do you think these convulsions of nature are accompanying political disturbances like they used to in Sartonius — Remember all the phenomena that surrounded Caesar and Augustus? Lightning and statues hurled down and all those augers. Well, I don't know — but it's funny we have a hurricane just while Hitler is starting to march.

— Katy Dos Passos to Sara Murphy, October 8, 1938

The Great Hurricane of 1938 was the worst weather disaster New England has ever experienced and the fourth-deadliest storm in U.S. history. In the number of lives lost, the amount of property damaged, and the breadth of the devastation, no other natural disaster in America's history came even close. Besides almost seven hundred lives, the hurricane claimed a centuries-old way of life.

"The greens and commons of New England will never be the same," the Associated Press reported. "Picture postcard mementos of the oldest part of the U.S. are gone with the wind and flood. The day of 'the biggest wind' has just passed, and a great part of the most picturesque America, as old as the Pilgrims, has gone beyond recall or replacement. New England's Revolutionary-rooted antiquity has been razed by the greatest nature-dealt disaster in its history."

The hurricane cost $4.7 billion in today's dollars. Some 93,000 families suffered serious property loss, and more than 19,000 families applied for emergency relief. Property losses were staggering, and only 5 percent were covered by insurance. Almost 20,000 buildings were wrecked, another 75,000 were damaged, and 26,000 cars were demolished.

The hurricane was an act of nature so devastating that in less than seven hours, it washed away dunes that had taken centuries to build and carved a new coastline. When the storm was over, the U.S. Coast and Geodetic Survey warned that existing maps of Long Island and New England were useless. New charts had to be drawn. The hurricane divided Jamestown into four parts, chopped Napatree into a series of small islands, and cut an eight-foot channel through Saltaire, Fire Island. It opened seven passages on Long Island, widening the Moriches Inlet and creating the Shinnecock Inlet. For years, residents of Hampton Bays had been debating whether to cut a channel from the bay to the ocean. The hurricane settled the question.

Surveying the stricken area, James L. Feiser, vice chairman of the Red Cross, said, "I have never seen a hurricane more complete in its devastation. I cannot recall any instances where whole communities were blown away and left a pile of splintered wreckage more than a mile from their original sites."

Westhampton Beach lost 153 houses, and most of those remaining were ruined. On Fire Island three hundred houses were swept away at Ocean Beach, one hundred at Fair Harbor, and one hundred at Saltaire. At Montauk one hundred houses were battered, and dozens of homeless families found shelter in the Montauk Manor, a summer hotel that was closed for the off-season.

In Massachusetts the shore of Buzzards Bay was little more than wreckage. One complete house was still standing in ritzy Westport Harbor. At Mattapoisett's Crescent Beach, of 107 cottages, a dozen remained. Horseneck Beach, Fairhaven, and Woods Hole were swept clean.

In South County the destruction was absolute. Ninety-nine percent of shoreline property from Quonochontaug to Charlestown, a distance of seven miles, was demolished. Some four hundred cottages at Misquamicut and almost two hundred on Charlestown Beach washed away. Charlestown Pond and Charlestown by the Sea lost another hundred homes, and Napatree was wiped off the map.

The value of beachfront property plummeted. The day after the hurricane, you could have bought a piece of land for ten cents, one old-timer said. In some places, property simply disappeared. Great Gull Island, the army's coastal artillery post between Long Island and Fisher's Island, shrank from eighteen acres to twelve in an afternoon. Three Rhode Island sisters who owned fifty shorefront acres on the twenty-first of September owned two acres on the twenty-second. According to the *Geographic Review*, erosion in a fierce hurricane can exceed the effects of a century of ordinary wave work.

Along the beaches, the handsome pavilions that had defined the shoreline with their gracious style and impeccable service were never rebuilt. "The pavilions were lovely things," a Rhode Island woman remembered. "It isn't what it used to be. We lost the pretty little shops like the very nice linen shops and things like that. What came in their place were pizza parlors and slot machine places, and nothing that was very attractive."

The economic decline that began in the Depression deepened. Mill towns that had been struggling never recovered. The very rivers that had powered them rose up and tore them down. Factories crumbled, and many of those still standing never reopened. What was left of New England's textile industry moved south, and once confident colonial towns became forlorn, little more than ghost towns.

Farmers lost more than 1,600 head of livestock and 750,000 chickens. Connecticut's tobacco production dropped from 15,000 acres to five. Trees that had stood in Revolutionary days were uprooted. Most of the Northeast's apple crop, three-quarters of Vermont's sugar maple trees, and half of New Hampshire's white pines were lost. The timber blown down was the equivalent of ten years' normal cut for that state. In Rhode Island, where white pines were the state's richest natural resource, a belt of lofty trees had stretched the length of the state, north to south. In three hours they were gone, and with them the state's entire lumber industry. The U.S. Forest Service estimated that there was enough hurricane timber to build 200,000 five-room houses — so much that sawing and salvaging it would take five years.

The fishing industry was also devastated. Maritime losses of all kinds were huge. Block Island lost thirty-six of its fifty-six fishing boats, and the rest were badly damaged. In Montauk, Long Island, more than eighty fishing boats were unsalvageable. In Stonington, fifty-three of the fifty-five-boat fleet were beyond repair. The *Gloria*, which was being overhauled in Bridgeport when the storm blew in, was the only smack working after the storm. In the afternoons fishing families would go down to the Stonington wharf when *Gloria* came in, and her captain would distribute the day's catch for free.

Besides their boats, fishermen lost equipment, miles of nets, and thousands of lobster pots. In Jerusalem and Galilee, Rhode

Island, pots as deep as 125 feet below the ocean surface and twenty-five miles out to sea were splintered. In one of the worst marine tolls, eighteen fishermen drowned when a pair of scallop-fishing boats out of Brooklyn, New York, sank off the coast of Nantucket.

Ferryboats took a beating, too. From Bridgehampton to Port Jefferson is a short hop — just twelve miles between the two Long Island towns. Ray Dickerson, captain of the passenger ferry *Park City*, had made the trip hundreds of times. He set out from Bridgehampton at two o'clock Wednesday afternoon with his usual nine-man crew and five passengers. The youngest was a two-month-old baby. The day was overcast and the wind strong, but the weather did not appear dangerous. Five miles out, in the middle of Long Island Sound, the wind began to howl and the sea boomed. The 150-foot steamer was heavy and powerful, but it might as well have been a cork. Captain Dickerson tried to turn back; the wind was too strong. He dropped anchor, thinking to ride out the storm; the anchor dragged. Torrents of water were flung across the decks and reached into the holds, dousing the boilers' fire and knocking out the generators. Before he could radio a distress signal, power, lights, and all communication were lost. The *Park City* floundered in the angry Sound. The next day a Coast Guard cutter spotted the ferry, battered but still afloat. All aboard were shaken but unharmed, including the baby, who, it was said, never cried. But Captain Ray Dickerson was haunted by the trip. He died the following year at the age of sixty-one.

The *Catskill*, another Long Island ferry, steamed out of Orient Point at 1:30 P.M. Wednesday afternoon, carrying a light, off-season load — just three cars and eight passengers. Captain Charles Sherman expected to cross the Sound and reach New London at 3:15 P.M. An hour out of port, high seas and hurricane winds began speeding the ferry toward Connecticut. The *Catskill* was on the last lap of its sixteen-mile trip when the captain realized that he would never be able to maneuver into New London harbor in such wild weather. The *Catskill* turned around and rode out the hurricane without ever losing power. Sometime in the night, when the winds and water calmed, the ferry resumed its trip. It reached New London at 10:30 P.M. By then, the city was in cinders and there was no longer a ferry dock.

In Jamestown the old *Beavertail*, the last of the wooden paddleboat ferries, had sailed her final voyage. She couldn't be salvaged from the rocks. The other Jamestown-to-Newport ferry, the *Governor Carr*, was sitting pretty on the front lawn of Webster Wetherill's house half a mile north of the ferry landing. Ladders were rigged to rescue the passengers (among them an admiral from the Newport Naval College and his wife). Once the water receded, there was a sizable expanse of dry land between the bay and the boat. Jamestown was in a quandary. Although the *Governor Carr* was unharmed, there was no way to get her back in the water. Eventually, the U.S. Army Corps of Engineers solved the dilemma by off-loading the cars that were still on board, then blasting a channel from the lawn through the rocks to the deep water of the bay. By New Year's, the *Governor Carr* was once again making the trip between the sister islands. She served Jamestown for nearly five decades. In the 1960s she was decommissioned and sold for scrap metal, and her hull was converted to a coal barge, an inglorious end to the era of Jamestown ferries.

The human and economic toll was measurable. The deepest impact of the hurricane was not. The swiftness and totality of the disaster were so stunning as to defy reason, logic, credulity. Social change evolves. Dunes and beaches and shorelines are shaped over a century of wind and wave. Lives and landscape require years of patient building, grain upon grain. They cannot be redrawn in two or three hours. On September 21, 1938, what couldn't happen did, and even for those who had been cushioned from the ravages of the Depression, life seemed suddenly fragile.

The vagaries of nature shook the status quo and weakened its underpinnings. On that rough September afternoon, wealth, social position, and property provided no buffer from the fury of wind and water. The comfort zone they had ensured would never seem quite as insular again. The hurricane has been called "a savage leveler." Chaos blew in, and in some ways it stayed on after the hurricane left town. The well-ordered life with distinct rules and classes came to an end, replaced by a world with new rules, new liberties, new equalities, and a new tempo. "Some line had been crossed," as Lee Davis put it, "and nothing would ever be quite the same again."

Although few, if any, realized it at the time, 1938 would be the last of the old New England summers. The Yankee establishment had been giving way slowly, so slowly that at first it wasn't recognized. A sea of newness was washing over it — a new deal, a square deal, a new social compact. The political and social changing of the guard. Rock-solid Republican states would become Democratic. As the changes begun with the New Deal accelerated, the pace of life began to quicken. Air travel, the only operable means of transportation, boomed. The week after the hurricane was the busiest ever in airline travel in the United States. With train service cut off, buses running sporadically, and roads obstructed, thousands took to the skies for the first time in their lives. American Airlines, which held exclusive rights to the New York–to–Boston corridor, could not meet the volume of traffic. Demand soared from two hundred passengers a day to one thousand. American had to invite TWA, United, and Eastern Airlines to join the route.

In the eight days following the storm, airlines carried 8,000 passengers and 37,000 pounds of mail. Some 60 percent of the passengers were first-time flyers who had been leery of leaving the ground. Once they got over their initial reluctance, flying became a favored mode of transportation. The surge in air travel that would continue for the rest of the century began with the hurricane.

To those who lived to tell the tale, more than any other single event, the hurricane marked the beginning of modern times. What nature's storm began, the storms of war would complete and a gracious, circumscribed way of life was lost forever.

In an area always resistant to change, culture, identity, and history were disrupted in a flash, and before New England could recover from the shock of the hurricane, there came a second terrible surprise: Pearl Harbor. Bad luck always comes in threes, they say. The Great Hurricane or 1938 was sandwiched between two national catastrophes. It came on the heels of the Great Depression and was followed by World War II. Almost to the day a year later, the storm troopers of the Third Reich marched into Poland.

Boys who survived the storm went off to war. Jim Nestor and Bill Chellis joined the navy. Clayton Chellis signed up, too, as soon as he was old enough, and when Geoffrey Moore finished prep school, he enlisted in the Marines. All four served in the Pacific. Jim was on the USS *Hornet* in 1942 when the aircraft carrier went down. He dove off the burning ship just in time. Geoffrey served with the Third Fleet. He was aboard the USS *Bonhomme Richard* that secured Tokyo Bay when General Douglas MacArthur received the Japanese surrender. When the war was over, Geoffrey enrolled in Harvard and, after graduation, went to work for his uncles at George C. Moore Co. Five years later he lit out on his own. Still athletic and vigorous today, he lives quietly in rural Pennsylvania with two massive mastiffs for company. His only child — a married daughter, Christine — lives in Germany.

Clayton served aboard the USS *Tarawa*. When the carrier was scheduled to return to the States, the sailors had a party on the beach at Saipan to celebrate. There was plenty to drink, probably too much. Clayton dove into the water. Eight years after he escaped death on the Jamestown school bus, he swam out past the reefs and was caught in an undertow. It was 1946 and he was nineteen.

Afterword

The island of Jamestown was altered irrevocably. From its founding, Jamestown could only be reached by boat. After the hurricane, the islanders' sense of isolation was so acute that within the year, a bridge was built connecting Jamestown to the mainland. The easier access altered the island's character, turning it from a self-contained rural community to a suburban development. Today, broad suspension bridges leapfrog Narragansett Bay, connecting Jamestown to the Rhode Island mainland on the one side and to Newport on the other. Even Beavertail, which hadn't changed much in three hundred years, became a different place. Before the hurricane it was open fields with sweeping sea views in every direction. The saline rains burned the grasslands that had attracted the founders to the island, and strange seeds borne on the winds changed the treeless beauty into a jungle of thick scrub that now shuts out the ocean views.

But at Fox Hill Farm, cows still graze in the pastures that slope down to the water. Children still learn to swim at Mackerel

Cove, where the surf is gentle, and cross the narrow causeway to dig for clams at Sheffield Cove. There is no memorial of the school bus tragedy there, no memory at all of the lost children.

Sixty-five years make a difference.

Out on Napatree at the edge of the ocean, a pair of sandpipers race the tide, darting after the ebbing water, then sprinting back before the ripple of waves can catch them. The birds are fast and small, so fast their black stick legs blur like ink lines, so light their feet leave only scratch marks on the sand. A third piper scurries down the beach, and the newly formed threesome skitters in and out with swift, dainty steps, like the three little maids from school in double time, triple time. Every movement is precise.

The beach is bare of shells, but there are stones, smooth and glistening, and a line of froth, like briny champagne bubbles, that the sea has left behind. The wet sand is marked with deep imprints from a fisherman's boots, and up where it is drier and softer, a black Lab sniffs at the ribbons of seaweed, once rubbery and slick, now brittle and dried into dullness. A tree trunk, forty or more feet long, lies sea-bleached and beached in the high sand. Beyond, where the beach crests, dune grass sways in an easy breeze.

On a perfect September afternoon, Napatree is empty except for the birds, the fisherman, and his dog. The smell of the sea is pungent. The ocean laps, deep green and docile. In the high, cerulean sky, made bluer by plump cumulus mattresses, the sun is a silver ball, and at the horizon, slivers of light reach down, touching the single sail that sits off the point and the buoy that marks the bay entrance.

It has become an annual September ritual to make the trek from Watch Hill to the old fort, to walk this barrier beach. It was an idyll, once, until a capricious Wednesday, at the ragtag end of summer, when a strange yellow light came off the ocean, an eerie, restless siren filled the air, and a world broke apart. A paradise was lost.

Fort Road is beach scrub now. On the ruined parapet of the old fort, details of the gun turrets, caserns, and bunkers are obscured by bayberry bushes and beach roses gone to autumn berries. Today there is no sign that Napatree was ever inhabited. Nothing to mark the spot where neighbors, friends, and families were lost and bodies were laid shoulder to shoulder. Napatree of 1938 has vanished without a trace.

On the walk back to Watch Hill, along the scythe of beach, it could be a different day. The sky is still blue to the west, but directly above, it is low and gunmetal gray, as if an awning has been drawn over the day. The ocean changes to green-black marble. The light on the Watch Hill Coast Guard Station flashes, suddenly ominous. The quick change in the weather is dramatic and unexpected — nature, like an accommodating host, offering a suggestion of what occurred here on September 21, 1938.

In her poem "We Have Seen the Wind: New England Hurricane, 1938," May Sarton wrote:

> *Do not speak to us any more of the carnage of the trees,*
> *Lest the heart remember other dead than these —*
> *Lest the heart split like a tree from root to crown,*
> *And bearing all its springs, like a feather go down.*

In this part of the country, where the past is always present, all that was lost may have gone without the sudden sea of September 1938. Or maybe not.

A Nickel for Your Story

After the storm had blown through, everyone in New England had a hurricane story and would repeat it so readily that an enterprising Boston man donned a sandwich board: FOR A NICKEL, I'LL LISTEN TO YOUR HURRICANE STORY. Here are a few of the strangest, saddest, or most amazing.

~ In the Westerly area, two babies, each one year old, rode out the storm safely on mattresses. One baby did not have a scratch or a sniffle. The other imbibed a quantity of seawater and spent several days in the Westerly Hospital on the critical list before making a full recovery.

~ A number of babies were born during the hurricane. Sergeant John Lipstack was stranded at his post in Fort Adams, Newport, while his wife was giving birth to a son at their apartment in Jamestown. On Long Island, Mrs. Joseph Gatz was doing well in what remained of Eastern Long Island Hospital. Her daughter, Shirley Ann, was born at 3:20 P.M., just as the hospital roof blew off and rain began pouring into the delivery room.

~ As if seeking payback for the generations of sailors guided safely home, the hurricane tore down lighthouses and cast the keepers and their families into the sea. In Narragansett Bay, the Castle Hill and Sandy Point lighthouses were badly damaged. The Sandy Point station house was swept away with keeper George T. Gustavas, his wife, his son, and three friends inside. A second wave tossed Gustavas back to shore, where he kept the light beaming throughout the storm. The Whale Rock Light, a solid cast-iron tower about a mile west of Beavertail Point, crashed down from its rocky base, taking the lightkeeper with it. At Bullock's Point Light in the Providence River channel, keeper Andrew Zaius climbed into the tower and kept the beacon lit even after the gale ripped off a wall and washed away the stairs.

~ Lightkeeper Arthur Small and his wife, Mabel, were alone on Palmer's Island near New Bedford, Massachusetts, that Wednesday. A modest man who often said that living in a city with fast cars and fast talkers was considerably more dangerous than keeping the Palmer Light shining, Captain Small had been keeper since 1919. As the day turned ominous, he told Mabel to wait in the oil house, the highest point on the island, while he rowed out to the light. His dinghy capsized in the churning sea. Mabel tried to launch a boat to rescue him. She died in the attempt, but Captain Small managed to swim to the lighthouse. He dragged himself into the tower and kept the light burning through the hurricane. In the morning, only two buildings were standing on Palmer's Island — the lighthouse and the oil house.

~ A crippled Mastick Beach, Long Island, man watched both of his artificial legs carried out of his cottage in the storm. Three days later they were found lying side by side on a beach at East Moriches, ten miles away.

~ At a farm in Mecox, Long Island, two cows were washed away in the storm surge. They swam home, clearing a four-foot wire fence, and showed up at the barn at the usual milking hour.

~ The Fo'c's'le, a favorite watering hole in Sakonnet Point, Rhode Island, was picked up, taken for a cruise, and dropped off on the other side of the point. The owner shored it up in its new location and opened for business as usual.

~ When WPRO, a Providence radio station, lost its transmitting tower, the manager connected the engine from a farmer's tractor to a power generator and resumed broadcasting.

~ Two teenagers, Charles Lucas and Tommy Fay, happened to be in the Quogue Market when a woman from Dune Road was offering a fifty-dollar reward to anyone who would go down to her house on Westhampton Beach and rescue her dog. The boys took the offer and set out just as the storm surge was rolling over the beach. Their bodies were found several days later.

~ Helen Lewis was scheduled to speak at a luncheon on Wednesday, September 21. She was the Republican nominee for secretary of state in Connecticut and the first woman ever nominated for statewide office. When the lunch was canceled at the last moment, Mrs. Lewis was thrilled. She could spend the perfect beach day with her husband and daughter at their home on Thimble Island, just off the coast of New London. Mrs. Lewis would not win the election. Her cottage was washed out to sea, and she and her husband drowned.

~ A wealthy Connecticut woman and her maid were rescued after riding out the storm atop her grand piano.

~ A Connecticut grandmother was found crushed beneath a large tree, clutching her grandson's rubbers. She went out at the height of the storm to meet the boy on his way home from school.

~ The First Lady of New York, Mrs. Fiorello La Guardia, was stranded upstairs in her Long Island home and rescued by firemen.

~ In Harrison, New York, "America's Sweetheart," Mary Pickford, narrowly escaped injury when a telephone pole fell on her car.

~ Three Misquamicut boys were trapped in a floating beach house when a neighboring cottage bumped up against theirs. An elderly woman was clinging to the roof. One boy with a rope tied around his waist attempted a rescue. He reached the woman, but her foot became wedged between the two houses. The boy was trying to free it when his friends shouted. A huge wave was about to break over the roof. They yanked the rope, pulling the boy back safely, but the woman was crushed.

~ The Sullivans, who operated a granite quarry in Westerly, owned a very sturdy house at Misquamicut, anchored with steel bars and reinforced with solid granite. Mrs. Sullivan was alone in the house during the hurricane. As the water rose, she went upstairs, finally holing up in the windowless attic, where she began to experience motion sickness. The attic was floating. Early the next morning, her husband and son found the attic on the far side of the salt pond. Mrs. Sullivan was inside, sound asleep on the couch.

~ Jack Tobin would fight in World War II, but his closest brush with death came in the storm. Tobin was getting out of his car when a slate shingle shot by, two inches from his neck, and buried itself in the steel of the car.

~ About one o'clock in the morning, twenty-seven-year-old Henry Morris of Weekapaug, Rhode Island, a carpenter and senior lifeguard, was searching for survivors when he saw a candle in a window of the Weekapaug Inn. Where the tennis courts had been the day before, there was now a ten-foot-deep, seventy-five-foot-wide breachway. The inn, or what remained of it, had become an island on which five people were trapped. The air was cold and the water was running fast, but Morris swam back and forth across the breachway five times and successfully rescued everyone at the inn. He received the Carnegie Medal for Heroism for his efforts.

~ As the epitome of an unflappable butler, Arni Benedictson proved to be the equal of Jeeves. Benedictson, the butler of Mr. and Mrs. William Ottman Jr., of Westhampton, sheltered twenty-three people during the storm, including the Countess Charles de Ferry de Fontnouvelle, wife of the French consul general, who had arrived at the Ottmans' door in her underwear, clutching her infant child. Benedictson rigged a flag from a bedsheet and waved it from the roof to signal for help. Deducing that their survival was precarious, he informed his guests that the situation was "most disturbing" and said, "Perhaps I should venture outside and bring help from the mainland." Benedictson struck out in the hurricane and returned with three "stout boys" in tow. With their help, he led his band to safety, shepherding them across a bridge to the mainland, just moments before the bridge collapsed.

~ Stanley Teller, chief of the two-man Westhampton Police Force, and his officer, Timothy Robinson, were trying to evacuate seventeen people from a beachfront house. Teller was carrying six-year-old twin boys out to his car when a huge wave swept up behind him and picked him up. He landed thirty feet in the air in the crossbar of a telephone pole. The twins vanished. While the chief was hanging on to the pole, Tim Robinson's rubber boots floated by — empty. They were distinctive boots: black rubber with white soles. The next thing Chief Teller remembered was floating in the bay on the roof of the house he had been evacuating. All seventeen people — including the twins and Officer Robinson — were riding on the roof with him.

~ On his 1939 IRS return, J. P. Morgan claimed $40,000 in repairs to the gardens of his Glen Cove, Long Island, estate.

~ Erselia Leah Griffin, a cook in Westhampton, had just been paid when the storm struck. In her rush to escape, she fell and dropped her purse. Although she reached safe ground, she was so upset about losing her full week's pay that she hunted through the wreckage for a solid week: "Finally, on a nice calm day about a week later, I found my purse back of the Quogue House Hotel, near where the help lived. There it was, my nice gray purse in the grass. The silver buckle glittered in the sun and caught my eye. The purse itself was barely damp and the money was completely dry."

~ When a Westhampton couple's house broke up, husband and wife went out on the roof. Then the roof split. They both went their separate ways, but ended up in a field side by side.

~ The windows of a Southold, Long Island, house were riddled with holes. What looked like sprays of machine-gun bullets were actually caused by horse chestnuts that gale winds had fired against the panes.

~ In a departure from the norm every bit as shocking as the arrival of a hurricane, the venerable Hope Club, an exclusively male bastion in Providence, opened its doors to both sexes for the first time. Hurricane or no hurricane, some old-time members reacted with shock and consternation, warning, "No good will come of it."

AUTHOR'S
ACKNOWLEDGMENTS

The knowledge, memories, and generosity of many went into *Sudden Sea*. Special thanks to my agent, F. Joseph Spieler, for never wavering; to my editor, Deborah Baker, for her perseverance and patience; to Alice B. Dwyer for her tenacious research; to Jane Burke O' Connell, Gloria Russell, and Scott Bill Hirst for their knowledge of the Westerly–Watch Hill area and its residents; to N. D. Scotti, Rhode Island historian, for his books and his learning; to Maria S. Chapin for charting the course; to Thomas F. Shevlin for his knowledge of ocean liners; to Joseph M. Scotti for his knowledge of Jamestown and all things nautical; to Carol A. Steel for her incisive reading; to Allison Markin Powell for her continued help and enthusiasm; to Stephen H. Lamont for his fine copyediting; and to Evans and Francesca Chigounis for their editorial acumen and forbearance.

I am also very grateful for the research help given by John T. Myers, city archivist, Providence, Rhode Island; Mary R. Miner, archivist, Jamestown Historical Society; Lynn Conway and Heather Bourk, archivists, Georgetown University; Tenley M. Chevalier, Alumni and Development Office, Tabor Academy; Andrew Morang, geologist, Coastal and Hydraulics Laboratory, Vicksburg, Mississippi; Elizabeth Middletown and John Palmieri, Herreshoff Museum, Bristol, Rhode Island; and Jack Williams and Bob Sheets, authors of *Hurricane Watch*.

Finally, thank you to William Rooney, George H. Utter, Douglas Steel, Dorothy and Thomas Stevens, Todd M. Chronister, Laura Katz Smith, Archives and Special Collections, Thomas J. Dodd Research Center, University of Connecticut, and William D. Caughlin, corporate archivist, SBC Communications Inc., for helping me with photographs.

SOURCES AND
CHAPTER NOTES

Instead of trying to relate every hurricane story, I have focused on a few experiences that seem representative of many more. My intention has not been to judge anyone caught in the storm, but rather to let the stories speak for themselves.

For the science of hurricanes and weather in general, I relied on a number of sources, particularly Gordon Dunn and Banner J. Miller's *Atlantic Hurricanes*, William K. Stevens's *The Change in the Weather*, Ivan Ray Tannehill's *Hurricanes: Their Nature and History*, and Ernest Zebrowski Jr.'s *Perils of a Restless Planet*.

For the story of this particular storm, I interviewed hurricane survivors, their families, and friends. Dozens of people, many of them strangers when I began to research the hurricane, gave generously of their time, knowledge, and memories. My thanks to: Dwight C. Brown Jr., Thomas Burke, Jane Moore Buffman, Mona Schmid Cavanaugh, Richard and William Chellis, Jayne Clarke, Fred Clarke, Lee Davis, John Whitman Davis, Helen and Irving Doyle, Catherine Moore Driscoll, Robert Driscoll, Bernard L.

Gordon, Dolores Matoes Hellewell, Ann Holst, Bernard Kenyon, Virginia Kershaw, Jack Kinney Jr., Judy Spicer Knutsen, William D. Metz, Geoffrey L. Moore Jr., Hatsy Moore, Marjorie Matoes Moran, James M. Nestor, Mary Vieira Ragland, Gretchen Greene Royce, Rita Dwyer Scotti, Patricia Driver Shuttleworth, Joanne Storrs, John D. Tobin, M.D., Patricia Miller Vandel, and Linda P. Woods.

Besides personal interviews with hurricane survivors, much of the information in this book was gleaned from the research facilities of the New-York Historical Society, the New York Society Library, the New York Public Library, the Jamestown Public Library, the Rhode Island Historical Society, the Newport Historical Society, the Westerly Public Library, the Langworthy Library in Hope Valley, the Southampton Public Library, and the National Archives, and from contemporary accounts in the *New York Times*, *New York Herald Tribune*, *Brooklyn Eagle*, *East Hampton News*, *Hartford Courant*, *Westerly Sun*, *Newport Daily News*, *Providence Journal-Bulletin*, and the *Boston Globe*.

I also drew from early books on the storm, most notably *A Wind to Shake the World* by Everett S. Allen, *Hurricane!* by Joe McCarthy, and *The 1938 Hurricane* by William Elliott Minsiner, M.D. Purely for narrative flow, I have occasionally condensed some quotes from previously published material.

The Hurricane in Rhode Island *In the Wake of '38*, interviews conducted in 1977 by students at the South Kingstown, Rhode Island, high school, was a great help in telling the Rhode Island stories. Descriptions of life on the island of Jamestown come from documents and publications of the Jamestown Historical Society. Information on the Matoes, Chellis, and Gianitis families comes from personal interviews with relatives, longtime island residents, and classmates. Norman Caswell's account of the school bus tragedy was published in the *Providence Evening Bulletin*. Joseph Matoes's account was published in *A Wind to Shake the World;* Clayton Chellis's story was related to me by his brothers William and Richard. In recounting the Napatree stories, I have relied on the accounts that survivors wrote for a special hurricane edition of the now defunct Watch Hill newspaper, *Seaside Topic*, as well as on the memories of friends and family members, particularly Geoffrey Moore, and Cathy Moore Driscoll, the only surviving family members who were alive in 1938, and Jim Nestor, now retired after a long career at Bostich and living in Ohio.

The Hurricane on Long Island   Mona Schmid Cavanaugh and Gretchen Greene Royce were wonderful sources. Patricia Driver Shuttleworth, who was a guest at the Greenes' unforgettable end-of-summer party and is now director of the Quogue, Long Island, Historical Society, kindly allowed me to quote from two books of memories she has compiled, *The 1938 Hurricane As We Remember It*, vols. 1 and 2. Among the contributors were Tot and Norvin Greene, who lived into their nineties, Arthur Raynor, and Lee Davis, now an author and teacher on Long Island. I am also indebted to Ernest S. Clowes and Roger K. Brickner for their detailed books on the impact of the 1938 Hurricane on Long Island and for the Long Island Express website of Scott A. Mandia, associate professor of physical science at the State University of New York, Suffolk.

Hepburn & Hughes   The account of Howard Hughes's flight is based on reports in the *New York Times, New York Herald Tribune, Time*, and *Life*, all from July 1938. The romance of Hepburn and Hughes and the account of Hepburn at her Fenwick family home are drawn from *Me*, Katharine Hepburn's autobiography, and from a number of biographies of both Hepburn and Hughes. (Please see Selected Bibliography for specific titles.) All quotes attributed to Katharine Hepburn come from *Me*.

The Bostonian   Recollections by passengers and crew of the
Bostonian train are drawn from several sources. Engineer Harry W.
Easton described the trip in *Railroad* magazine, July 1942. Easton
and the conductor, Joseph Richards, and several passengers gave
interviews to Joe McCarthy for *Hurricane!* Lawrence Burwell wrote
his account of the trip in a special freshman issue of the *Brown University
Herald* in September 1938.

U.S. Weather Bureau   Information on the Weather Bureau in
1938, including all correspondence and memos cited here, come
from the records of the U.S. Weather Bureau, now housed in the
National Archives in Silver Spring, Maryland.

—— SPECIFIC NOTES

Prologue: Gone with the Wind

When Hughes completed his record-setting round-the-world
flight, New York threw a huge ticker-tape parade. More than 1.5
million New Yorkers lined the steel-and-concrete canyon. A blizzard
of paper — 1,800 tons of shredded phone books, newspapers, and
ticker tape — poured from office windows. The *New York Times*
reported that "only the hot July sun kept the scene from resembling
a snowstorm."

"The most totally magnetic woman . . ." quote from *Howard
Hughes: The Untold Story* by Peter Harry Brown and Pat H. Broeske;
David O. Selznick quote from *Kate: The Life of Katharine Hepburn* by
Charles Higham.

Chapter 1: A Perfect Day

Jamestown is also known by its Indian name, Conanicut Island,
after the revered Narragansett chief. I have used the name Beavertail to refer to the entire southwestern section, not just the southern
tip of the island, because that is how the area is known today. The
large island across Narragansett Bay, which includes Newport,

Portsmouth, Middletown, and Bristol, is Aquidneck Island, or Isle of Peace.

Oddly enough, the Moores and the Matoeses both lived on roads that ended at nearly identical forts built by George Washington Goethals before he went off to work on the Panama Canal — Fort Mansfield on Napatree, Fort Getty on Jamestown. The fortifications were built to guard Little Narragansett Bay and Narragansett Bay proper from an illusory invasion. At the time of the Spanish-American War, fear of an attack was whipped up in the notorious yellow journals of William Randolph Hearst and Joseph Pulitzer. During World War II, Fort Getty was used as a camp for German prisoners of war.

"Sunshine, surf, and salt air . . ." quote from *The Search* by Paul Moore, whose sister Havila and stepmother, Jessie, died in the storm.

Information on Westerly's history comes from *Westerly and Its Witnesses* by the Reverend Frederic A. Denison.

Information on the deadly force of extreme hurricanes comes from Nigel Calder's *The Weather Machine*, A. B. C. Whipple's *Storm*, and Gordon Dunn's *Atlantic Hurricanes*.

In Providence, Rhode Island, the official water level on the Old Market House is 13.85 feet; however, according to contemporary reports, water reached 17 feet in some streets.

Chapter 2: The Way It Was

William Manchester's *The Glory and the Dream*, articles and advertisements in contemporary newspapers and magazines, and the recollections of many who lived through the 1930s helped me imagine the period.

Chapter 3: A Shift in the Wind

Information on the power of hurricanes comes from Gordon Dunn's *Atlantic Huricanes*, Ivan Ray Tannehill's *Hurricanes: Their Nature and History*, and A. B. C. Whipple's *Storm*.

Chapter 4: Hurricane Watch

Grady Norton continued to man the Jacksonville Hurricane Center through the 1940s and oversaw the establishment of the Hurricane Hunters aerial reconnaissance. He died on the job, while tracking Hurricane Hazel in 1954. The following year the National Hurricane Center was established, and Gordon Dunn was named its director. Dunn wrote *Atlantic Hurricanes*, which became a classic in the field, and traveled around the world helping other nations establish modern weather services. Profiles of Norton and Dunn were written by Robert Burpee in *Weather and Forecasting*. Norton was also profiled in *Life* magazine in 1948. The "By the time you wrestle with one of these big blows . . ." quote comes from that interview.

Chapter 5: At Sea

Information on Ernesto Gherzi, S.J., the Jesuit forecasters, and the SS *Conte di Savoia* comes from an interview Father Gherzi gave to the *Washington Herald* the week after the hurricane; the on-line *Catholic Encyclopedia*, the Georgetown University archives, David Longshore's *Encyclopedia of Hurricanes, Typhoons, and Cyclones*, the passenger log of the *Conte di Savoia*, and the Lido Line website.

Regarding Captain Greig and the RMS *Carinthia*, I drew from the Cunard Line archives, University of Liverpool Library, and *Pictorial Encyclopedia of Ocean Liners 1860–1994*, by William H. Miller (New York: Dover Publications, 1995).

"Whenever I have a difficult challenge . . ." quote from Robert Burpee's interview.

Chapter 6: All Aboard

The letter to Fred Moore is reprinted from *The Search* by his son Paul.

Chapter 7: A Bright Young Man

Charles Pierce wrote about the storm in the *Monthly Weather Review* in the summer of 1939. Additional information comes from a number of weather books, including Longshore's *Encyclopedia of Hurricanes, Typhoons, and Cyclones*.

Regarding the advanced meteorology in Europe: Adopting World War I terminology, Norwegian meteorologists pictured the atmosphere as a vast battleground with distinct fronts and warring weather systems. The Norwegians showed that most storms develop along the boundaries, or fronts, between huge air masses with different temperatures.

Information on the Great September Gale of 1815 comes from David Ludlum's *Early American Hurricanes 1492–1870* and Sidney Perley's *Historic Storms of New England*.

Chapter 10: A One-Hundred-Year Storm

"The plane flew through bursts of . . ." quote from "Hurricanes" by Robert Simpson in *Scientific American*, June 1954; "A unique and strangely tinted day . . ." quote from Howard E. Smith Jr.'s *Killer Weather*; "In the morning it was beautiful, . . ." "I had to crawl . . . ," and "It's a hurricane . . ." quotes from *In the Wake of '38*.

Chapter 11: How Do You Lose a Hurricane?

Regarding Cole Porter's new show, Richard Watts spoke for all the critics who braved the night when he wrote in the *Herald Tribune*: "The first musical show of the new season hardly adds distinction to that interesting branch of the dramatic art."

Chapter 12: The Long Island Express

Letter from Gerald Murphy from *Letters from the Lost Generation*, edited by Linda Patterson Miller.

Chapter 13: Crossing the Sound

The storm at Tabor Academy comes from *The School and the Sea: A History of Tabor Academy* by Joseph J. Smart.

Chapter 15: The Dangerous Right Semicircle

The history of the state is drawn from *A Short History of Rhode Island* by George W. Greene and from publications of the Jamestown Historical Society. It should be noted that Rhode Island is a small world. As one notable local historian put it, "Every Yankee in the state is related to an Arnold." The same family names turn up repeatedly. The Cottrells sold their Jamestown land to Philip Caswell. Members of the same family were living at Fox Hill Farm in 1938 and rented the meadows to Joe Matoes, and Violet Cottrell, who was playing golf with Harriet Moore on the afternoon of the hurricane.

Regarding barrier beaches: Early settlers were quick to recognize the instability of barrier islands, and few of them were foolhardy enough to build a permanent settlement on these shifting piles of sand. In 1838, however, a group of investors formed the Galveston City Company and began dividing the real estate of Galveston Island, a barrier island near Houston, Texas. By 1900, when the terrible Galveston hurricane struck, a single five-block span of mansions boasted twenty-six millionaires.

Chapter 16: Providence

David Cornel de Jong wrote his description of the hurricane for the September 1939 issue of *Yankee* magazine. The damage to the original Brown University charter was described in an article in *Brown University Alumni Magazine*, November–December 2001. Hartley Ward's account of the storm is taken from a privately printed pamphlet in the collection of the Newport Historical Society.

Chapter 17: The Tempest

C. W. Magruder's "Everyone expected . . ." quote was drawn from a document in the Jamestown Historical Society; "with three blasts of her horn . . ." quote also taken from a document in the Jamestown Historical Society.

Regarding the Colonial Hurricane of 1635: Besides the accounts of Governors Winthrop and Bradford, I drew from two nineteenth-century books, Increase Mather's *Remarkable Providences* and Sidney Perley's *Historic Storms of New England,* and from David Ludlum's *Early American Hurricanes 1492–1870.*

A couple of interesting historical notes: Many of our Founding Fathers were keen weather watchers. The early colonial governors Winthrop and Bradford filled their journals with detailed notations about the weather; Washington and Jefferson kept weather journals; and Benjamin Franklin's observations were significant. Also, when the *James* out of Bristol lost her anchors and sails and was blown within a cable's length of the rocks off Pastacaquack in the Colonial Hurricane, there were 100 passengers aboard, including the Reverend Richard Mather, who would father Increase Mather, who would recount the tale of Thacher's Woe in his book *Remarkable Providences.*

Chapter 18: Cast Adrift

"They came neck deep . . ." quote from the September 1939 *Yankee* magazine.

Chapter 20: The Reckoning

Statistics compiled from the figures of the National Weather Service, the Red Cross, the WPA, the New England Power Association, the Southern New England Telephone Company, and the New York, New Haven & Hartford Railroad Company. "Devastation everywhere . . ." quote from *The 1938 Hurricane As We Remember It,* vol. 1.

Chapter 21: The Last of the Old New England Summers

Letter from Katy Dos Passos from *Letters from the Lost Generation,* edited by Linda Patterson Miller. Statistics compiled from the figures of the National Weather Service, the Red Cross, and the WPA. Quote from the vice chairman of the Red Cross appeared in the *Newport* (R.I.) *Daily News* on October 1, 1938.

Appendix: A Nickel for Your Story

The stories were recounted in interviews or published in contemporary newspaper accounts of the hurricane.

Photograph Credits

Beach Erosion Board Archives, courtesy of the Coastal and Hydraulics Laboratory, U.S. Army Corps of Engineers, Vicksburg, MI.

National Oceanic and Atmospheric Administration Photo Library, Historic National Weather Service Collection (pp. 3, 12, 13 bottom).

National Oceanic and Atmospheric Administration Photo Library, Historic National Weather Service Collection, photo by Steve Nicklas (pp. 10, 13 top, 14).

Southern New England Telephone Company Records, Archives and Special Collections at the Thomas J. Dodd Research Center, University of Connecticut Libraries.

SELECTED
BIBLIOGRAPHY

—— BOOKS

Allen, Everett S. *A Wind to Shake the World*. Boston: Little, Brown, 1976.

Baker, Paul R. *Stanny: The Gilded Life of Stanford White*. New York: Free Press, 1989.

Baldwin, Charles C. *Stanford White*. New York: Da Capo Press, 1976.

Barlett, Donald L., and James B. Steele. *Empire: The Life, Legend, and Madness of Howard Hughes*. New York: W. W. Norton, 1976.

Bennett, Jackie Parlato. *The 1938 Hurricane As We Remember It*. Vol. 2. East Patchogue, N.Y.: Searles Graphics Inc., 1998.

Bowditch, Nathaniel. *Waves, Wind, and Weather*. New York: David McKay, 1977.

Bradford, William. *Of Plimouth Plantation, 1620–1647*. New ed. New York: Knopf, 1952.

Brickner, Roger K. *The Long Island Express: Tracking the Hurricane of 1938*. Batavia, N.Y.: Hodgins Printing Co., 1988.

Brown, Peter Harry, and Pat H. Broeske. *Howard Hughes: The Untold Story*. New York: Dutton, 1996.

Calder, Nigel. *The Weather Machine.* New York: Viking, 1974.

Chenoweth, James. *Oddity Odyssey.* New York: Henry Holt, 1996.

Clowes, Ernest. *The Hurricane of 1938 on Eastern Long Island.* Bridgehampton, N.Y.: Hampton Press, 1939.

Conforti, Joseph A. *Imagining New England.* Chapel Hill, N.C.: University of North Carolina Press, 2001.

Conrad, Joseph. *Typhoon and Other Tales.* New York: Oxford University Press, 1998.

Denison, Rev. Frederic A. *Westerly and Its Witnesses.* Providence: J. A. & R. A. Reid, 1878.

Dunn, Gordon E., and Banner J. Miller. *Atlantic Hurricanes.* Baton Rouge: Louisiana State University Press, 1960.

Edwards, Anne. *Katharine Hepburn: A Remarkable Woman.* New York: St. Martin's Press, 2000.

Gordon, Bernard L., ed. *Hurricane in Southern New England.* Watch Hill, R.I.: Book & Tackle Shop, 1996.

Greene, George W. *A Short History of Rhode Island.* Providence: J. A. & R. A. Reid, 1877.

Hack, Richard. *Hughes: The Private Diaries, Memos and Letters.* Beverly Hills: New Millennium Press, 2001.

Hendrickson, Richard G. *Winds of the Fish's Tail.* Mattituck, N.Y.: Amereon Ltd., 1996.

Hepburn, Katharine. *Me: Stories of My Life.* New York: Knopf, 1991.

Higham, Charles. *Kate: The Life of Katharine Hepburn.* New York: W. W. Norton, 1975.

Howard, John M. *100 Years in Jamestown: From Destination Resort to Bedroom Town.* Jamestown, R.I.: Jamestown Historical Society, 2000.

Hughes, Patrick. *A Century of Weather Service: A History of the Birth and Growth of the National Weather Service, 1870–1970.* New York: Gordon and Breach, 1970.

Selected Bibliography

Kahl, Jonathan D. *Weatherwise*. Minneapolis: Lerner Publications Co., 1992.

Laskin, David. *The Stormy History of American Weather*. New York: Doubleday, 1996.

Lippincott, Bertram. *Jamestown Sampler*. Flourtown, Pa.: GO Printing Corp., 1980.

Longshore, David. *Encyclopedia of Hurricanes, Typhoons, and Cyclones*. New York: Checkmark Books, 2000.

Ludlum, David. *Early American Hurricanes, 1492–1870*. Boston: American Meteorological Society, 1963.

Manchester, William Raymond. *The Glory and the Dream: A Narrative History of America, 1932–1972*. Boston: Little, Brown, 1974.

Mather, Increase. *Remarkable Providences: Illustrative of the Early Days of American Colonisation*. London: Reeves and Turner, 1890.

McCarthy, Joe. *Hurricane!* New York: American Heritage Press, 1969.

Miller, Linda Patterson, ed. *Letters from the Lost Generation: Gerald and Sara Murphy and Friends*. New Brunswick: Rutgers University Press, 1991.

Minsinger, William Elliott, M.D., ed. *The 1938 Hurricane: An Historical and Pictorial Summary*. Randolph Center, Vt.: Green Hill Books, 1988.

Moore, Paul J. *The Search: An Account of the Fort Road Tragedy*. Westerly, R.I.: Sun Graphics, 1988.

Nebeker, Frederik. *Calculating the Weather: Meteorology in the 20th Century*. San Diego: Academic Press, 1995.

Nese, John M., and Lee M. Grenci, eds. *A World of Weather: Fundamentals of Meteorology*. Dubuque, Iowa: Kendall/Hunt, 1998.

Peck, Reginald. *Early Landholders of Watch Hill*. Westerly, R.I.: Utter Company, 1936.

Peirce, Neal R. *The New England States*. New York: W. W. Norton, 1976.

Perley, Sidney. *Historic Storms of New England.* Salem, Mass.: Salem Press Publishing and Printing Company, 1891.

Reynolds, Ross. *Cambridge Guide to the Weather.* Cambridge: Cambridge University Press, 2000.

Rhode Island Committee for the Humanities and South Kingstown High School. *In the Wake of '38: Oral History Interviews with Rhode Island Survivors and Witnesses of the Devastating Hurricane of September 21, 1938.* Wakefield, R.I.: n.p., 1977.

Rhode Island Historical Preservation and Heritage Commission. *Historical and Architectural Resources of Jamestown, Rhode Island.* Providence: Rhode Island Historical Society, 1995.

Rhode Island Historical Society. *What a Difference a Bay Makes.* Providence: Rhode Island Historical Society, 1993.

Sheets, Bob, and Jack Williams. *Hurricane Watch.* New York: Vintage Books, 2001.

Shirer, William. *The Rise and Fall of the Third Reich.* New York: Simon & Schuster, 1990.

Shuttleworth, Patricia D. *The 1938 Hurricane As We Remember It.* Vol. 1. East Patchogue, N.Y.: Searles Graphics Inc., 1998.

Smith, Howard E. *Killer Weather: Stories of Great Disasters.* New York: Dodd, Mead, 1982.

Stevens, William K. *The Change in the Weather: People, Weather, and the Science of Climate.* New York: Delacorte Press, 1999.

Tannehill, Ivan Ray. *Hurricanes: Their Nature and History.* Rev. ed. Princeton, N.J.: Princeton University Press, 1952.

U.S. Weather Bureau Records, Record Group 0027, National Archives Building, Silver Spring, Md.

Ward, A. Hartley G. *The Hurricane in Newport.* Privately printed, 1938.

Watson, Benjamin A. *Acts of God: The Old Farmer's Almanac — Unpredictable Guide to Weather and Natural Disasters.* New York: Random House, 1993.

Whipple, A.B.C. *Storm*. Alexandria, Va.: Time-Life Books, 1982.

Wilder, Thornton. *Theophilus North*. New York: Avon Books, 1973.

Winthrop, John. *The History of New England 1630 to 1649*. Boston: Little, Brown, 1853.

Wright, Catherine Moore. *The Portuguese of Conanicut Island: History through Memories*. Privately printed, 1980.

Zebrowski, Ernest Jr. *Perils of a Restless Planet*. Cambridge: Cambridge University Press, 1997.

—— 1938 NEWSPAPER SUPPLEMENTS AND PRIVATELY PRINTED BOOKLETS

Complete Record of New England's Stricken Area. New Bedford (MA) *Standard Times, Morning Mercury*.

Complete Record of New England's Stricken Area. Woonsocket (RI) *Call*.

The Devastation and Restoration of New England's Vital Life-Line: The New Haven Railroad. New York, New Haven & Hartford Railroad Company.

Flood and Hurricane Issue. New England Power Association.

The Great Hurricane and Tidal Wave of Rhode Island. Providence Journal Co., 1938.

The Hurricane and Flood of September 21, 1938, at Providence, R.I. Pictorial Record Bristol, 1938.

Hurricane and Flood of 1938. Southern New England Telephone Company.

The Hurricane of 1938, Westerly, by William Cawley.

The Hurricane, Sept. 21, 1938, by Lewis R. Greene.

Hurricane Tidal Wave, Charlestown (1938).

New England Hurricane. Federal Writers' Project, 1938.

Watch Hill in the Hurricane of September 21, 1938. Charles Hammond, ed., *Seaside Topics*, Watch Hill, R.I.

—— NEWSPAPERS AND PERIODICALS

Boston Globe, September 1938.

Brooklyn Eagle, September 1938.

Easthampton (LI) *Star*, September 1938.

Hartford Courant, September 1938, September 1988.

Life, July–October 1938.

Newport Daily News, September 1938.

New York Herald-Tribune, July–September 1938.

New York Sun, September 1938.

New York Times, July–September 1938.

Providence Journal-Bulletin, September 1938, September 1988.

Tidings, August 1988 (Hurricane Issue).

Time, July–October 1938.

Westerly (RI) *Sun*, September 1938, September 1988.

Yankee, September 1939 (Hurricane Issue).

—— WEBSITES

www.pbs.org/wgbh/amex/hurricane38   The American Experience: The Hurricane of 1938.

www2.sunysuffolk.edu/mandias/38hurricane The Long Island Express

www.aoml.noaa.gov

www.greatoceanliners.net/contedisavoia

—— ARTICLES

"The Atlantic Hurricanes" by Edward N. Rappaport and Avila A. Lixion, *Weatherwise*, February–March 1995.

"Big Wind Man" by J. Kobler, *Life*, October 4, 1948.

"Engineering Aspects of the New England Hurricane of 1938" by James A. Grant, *The Military Engineer* 31, no. 176, March–April 1939.

"The Geography of Hurricanes," *National Geographic*, September 1980.

"Geography of a Hurricane," *National Geographic*, April 1939.

"Gordon E. Dunn: Preeminent Forecaster of Midlatitude Storms and Tropical Cyclones" by Robert Burpee, *Weather and Forecasting*, December 1989.

"Grady Norton: Hurricane Forecaster and Communicator Extraordinaire" by Robert Burpee, *Weather and Forecasting*, September 1988.

"Hurricane Hazard in New England," *Geographical Review*, January 1939.

"Hurricane Modification of the Off-Shore Bar of Long Island, New York" by Arthur David Howard, *Geographical Review*, 1939.

"Hurricanes" by Robert Simpson, *Scientific American*, June 1954.

"Hurricanes and Shore-Line Changes in Rhode Island" by Charles W. Brown, *Geographical Review* 29, 1939.

"Hurricanes in New England" by Charles F. Brooks, *Geographical Review* 29, December 1939.

"The Meteorological History of the New England Hurricane of Sept. 21, 1938" by Charles H. Pierce, *Monthly Weather Review* 67, August 1939.

"The Recent Hurricane in New England" by Ivan Ray Tannehill, *Scientific Monthly*, January 1939.

"The Siege of New England" by Hugh D. Cobb III, *Weatherwise*, October 1939.

"Storms of the Century," *Weatherwise* 48, June–July 1995.

"Wind and Fury" by Frances Woodward, *Atlantic Monthly*, December 1938.

"Winds and Pressures over the Sea in the Hurricane of September 1938," *Monthly Weather Review* 84, no. 7, July 1956.

INDEX

ABOUT THE AUTHOR

R. A. Scotti grew up in Rhode Island hearing stories about the Great Hurricane of 1938. She is the author of numerous thrillers and novels of international espionage and is a former journalist at the *Providence Journal* and *Newark Star-Ledger*. This is her second work of nonfiction.